P9-DFH-643

# Christian Counseling and the Law

Steve Levicoff

MOODY PRESS
CHICAGO

The use of selected references from various versions of the Bible in this publication does not necessarily imply publisher endorsement of the versions in their entirety.

The information contained herein is general in nature and should not be construed as legal advice. It is sold with the understanding that the neither the publisher nor the author is engaged in rendering legal or other professional service. If legal advice is required, the services of a competent attorney should be sought.

**Library of Congress Cataloging in Publication Data**

Levicoff, Steve.
Christian counseling and the law / by Steve Levicoff.
p. cm.
Includes bibliographical references and index.
ISBN 0-8024-1239-4
1. Pastoral counseling—Law and legislation—United States.
2. Clergy—Legal status, laws, etc.—United States. I. Title.
KF4868.C44L38 1991
346.7303'3—dc20
[347.30633] 90-28073
CIP

1 2 3 4 5 6 7 8 Printing/AK/Year 95 94 93 92 91

*Printed in the United States of America*

*In memory of*
*Lynne Ardis Smith*

**What You Don't Know *Can* Hurt You**

Do you know:

What constitutes "clergy malpractice" and "negligent counseling"?
What is "duty of care"?
When do you break confidentiality?
When are you breaking the law?
What are the legal ramifications of church discipline?
What is your responsibility in child abuse cases?
Can you use counseling illustrations in your sermons?

If you are a pastor or counselor, or are in any counseling ministry, this may be the most important new book you will read this year.

In this "age of litigation" an explosive new area of law—suing churches—is impacting Christians. How do these lawsuits affect pastors and counselors?

Steve Levicoff's scholarly, yet easy to read, *Christian Counseling and the Law*, summons all Christian counselors to study the law themselves so that they can be "as shrewd as serpents and as innocent as doves" and thereby "fight the good fight of faith" in the secular arena.

This is not a book filled with stilted legalese and lofty phrases. It is a straightforward, well-documented resource for the Christian counselor. When you put it down—if you can—you will probably say, "That was just what I needed."

**About the Author**

**Steve Levicoff**, Visiting Lecturer in Law, Biblical Theological Seminary, Hatfield, Pennsylvania, holds the M.A. in Theology and Law from Vermont College of Norwich University and earned his Ph.D. in Religion and Law from the Union Institute, Cincinnati, Ohio. He resides in Plymouth Meeting, Pennsylvania, and is the author of *Building Bridges: The Prolife Movement and the Peace Movement.*

The sad truth is that Christian counseling has become a legal and constitutional mine field upon which even angels fear to tread. In *Christian Counseling and the Law* my good friend Dr. Steve Levicoff has written a very readable and practical book that could quite literally save your neck. Steve combines his knowledge of law, counseling, and theology to give us a book that no Christian counselor should be without.

JOHN EIDSMOE, J.D., M.DIV., D.MIN.
Professor of Constitutional Law
Jones School of Law
Faulkner University

# Contents

# Foreword

When I was preparing for my career as a professional counselor my mind was consumed with philosophical questions: Why does depression exist? What role does spirituality play in emotional health? What causes some to be compatible marital partners and others not? How can a person overcome a dreadful family history to lead a productive Christian life? How can persons communicate sound biblical beliefs without being legalistic?

Within the past generation we have seen a rise in the acceptability of Christian counseling. Christian professionals in private clinics are trained to help hurting persons sift through such challenging questions while maintaining a commitment to the infallible authority of Scripture. Much good is arising from the increasing awareness that Christian counseling is a viable alternative to humanistic psychology.

But professional counselors are not alone in responding to the demands of a hurting public. Long before the profession of counseling became popular, pastors and church leaders led the way for those seeking to apply God's truth to everyday life. In fact, more counseling has actually been done by church people helping one another than by all the combined efforts of the professional counselors. Paul admonished the first generation church to bear one another's burdens, thus fulfilling the law of Christ, and the church has been doing so for two milleniums.

In my years of counseling, though, and through my close association with many clergy and lay counselors, I have learned that there is more to be concerned about than merely communicating truth to those seeking spiritual guidance. In today's litigious society we have had to become cautious regarding the many possibilities for legal action. Pastors, prayer group leaders, Bible study teachers, and even church secretaries are learning that great caution must be exercised in the ministry lest any deviation from societal norms be construed as neglectful or harmful to another. Virtually all Christians are in agreement with the biblical mandate to live within "Caesar's" guidelines. But the question often arises: "Exactly what are the boundaries that apply to Christians who are called upon to assist individuals seeking God's will for their lives?"

I am most grateful to Steve Levicoff for the way he has helped the Christian community decipher the legal boundaries that apply to Christian ministries. Using case examples and citing legal precedents, he makes clear that which otherwise might be confounding. He specifically spells out what constitutes confidentiality, when to defer to medical personnel, when to involve the family, and many other pertinent issues. After reading this book, the Christian counselor should have a clear direction in those delicate issues that require a careful understanding of the counselee's rights and the counselor's responsibilities.

I know that the desire of most Christians is to be a conduit of God's grace to those in genuine need. By guiding us through the intricacies of the legal maze, Steve Levicoff has made it easier for Christian leaders to do what God has commanded without a cloud of doubt hanging overhead.

LES CARTER, PH.D.
Minirth-Meier Clinic
Dallas, Texas

# Preface

There was a time when churches, not to mention Christians themselves, enjoyed the respect of society and practiced a ministry undiluted by concerns other than spreading the gospel, speaking honestly about social and political ills from a scriptural perspective, and helping those who sought counsel with an emphasis on following sound biblical doctrine. But times have changed, and when pastors and Christian counselors pursue their ministries, the nagging question in the back of their mind is, "How will this affect me legally?"

Churches, ministries, and individual pastors and counselors are being sued from within as well as from outside the Body of Christ. This book discusses how to avoid lawsuits and considers the legal ramifications of the Christian counseling ministry, both within the pastorate and in terms of lay counselors and professional Christian counseling centers.

Yet there are instances in which litigation should, perhaps, not be avoided. There will be times when a pastor or counselor should follow scriptural principles, even at the risk of being sued. Jesus gives a pointed reminder:

> Which one of you, when he wants to build a tower, does not first sit down and calculate the cost, to see if he has enough to complete it? Otherwise, when he has laid a foundation, and is not able to finish, all who observe it begin to ridicule him, saying, "This man began to build and was not able to finish." Or

> what king, when he sets out to meet another king in battle, will not first sit down and take counsel whether he is strong enough with ten thousand men to encounter the one coming against him with twenty thousand? (Luke 14:28-32)

There may be times when the cost of referring a believer to a secular counselor is too high or when allowing an errant member to continue in fellowship without church discipline disrupts the congregation more than the discipline itself, even though pursuing the safer course of action from a civil perspective may avoid a lawsuit.

I do not pretend to have easy answers to these dilemmas, but I do believe that in a situation where one must choose between God's law and man's law, we should not only count the cost but be prepared to deal with the ramifications. In other legal situations, there is no conflict between biblical principles and civil law. Yet as counselors, our ministries will be most secure when we know how to act within the law.

This is not the first book written on the law as it impacts counselors. However, the few volumes that do exist are geared toward secular counselors, psychologists, and psychiatrists. Consequently they do not address the specific issues that affect Christian counseling. At the same time, many books written from the secular counseling perspective are antagonistic not only toward religion in general but toward biblical Christianity in particular.

Most readers are familiar with the old expression "I read the end of the Book, and we win." As Christians, the Scriptures tell us that we'll win the war. But there will be some tough battles ahead, both in and out of the courtroom.

This book, then, is a basic guide on how the law affects counselors who operate from a Christian counseling framework. It is not intended to be a substitute for legal counsel, but after reading it the counselor will hopefully be aware of how to deal with the potential legal impact of many counseling situations. Nonetheless, a caveat is appropriate here: for specific legal problems, competent legal counsel should be retained.

I am indebted to several colleagues and mentors who commented on the draft of this volume, especially William Durland, John Eidsmoe, Dennis Huber, and Cathi Walsh-Haehle. Individual chapters were also reviewed by Carol Hurley, Charles Maresca, Stephen Matthews, and Ken Sande, all of whom provided valuable feedback. I am also grateful for the counsel of Pastor Ernest Mascho of Grace Baptist Church and the faculty and students of Biblical Theological Seminary, especially Joanna Hause, James Pakala, Frederic Putnam, and Charles Zimmerman. Finally, I am indebted to Jim Bell, R. Duncan Jaenicke, Joe O'Day, and the staff of Moody Press for their support and assistance in the production of this volume. Nonetheless, the subjective conclusions herein are my own, and for them I take full responsibility.

# 1

# The Dispensation of Litigation?

A few years ago, I conducted a radio interview with a prominent social activist. During our talk, she commented, "Just because a person's paranoid doesn't mean there's not a reason to be."

When I returned to my home in the Philadelphia area after a graduate semester in California, I noticed a change in the weekly bulletin of my local church. The Sunday bulletin always included a coupon that visitors could remove and place in the offering plate. In addition to a space for the visitor's name, address, and phone number, the form had several items that could be checked off. It looked like this:

I am interested in:

____ Receiving Jesus Christ
____ Prayer Chain
____ Being Baptized
____ Helping with the Children's Ministry
____ Prayer for ________________________
____ Hospitality Ministry
____ Being Counseled
____ Home Fellowships
____ Other ___________________________

With no public announcement made and little notice by the members, the line labeled "Being Counseled" was replaced by the words "Speaking with a Pastor." After a few months, there was yet another change. "Speaking with a Pastor" was replaced by "Talking with an Elder."

Over the past few years, many churches around the nation have dropped their counseling ministries, reasoning that the risk of lawsuits is too great to continue offering counseling services. Are they simply being paranoid? Perhaps. But then, just because you're paranoid doesn't mean there's not a reason to be.

The chance that a church will be sued for clergy malpractice, negligent counseling, or any other type of professional negligence is small. If we hypothetically assume that the incidence of pastors or counselors who will be sued for professional malpractice in the course of their careers is 1 percent, that might still be a large estimate.[1] Yet to the individual pastor or counselor who experiences a lawsuit, percentages are meaningless.

## Background to the *Nally* Case

The current concern about clergy malpractice started with the case of *Nally v. Grace Community Church of the Valley.*[2] Although many pastors and counselors are already familiar with the case, a review of the basic events will help delineate the dilemma facing Christian counselors today.

On April 1, 1979, twenty-four-year-old Kenneth Nally committed suicide by shooting himself in the head with a shotgun. Ken had been born and raised a Roman Catholic, and

1. It is too early to predict trends in the rates of litigation for counseling malpractice suits against pastoral, or Christian, counselors. Comparing with the secular area, however, only an estimated 0.5 percent of psychologists insured by the American Psychological Association Insurance Trust have been sued over a fourteen-year average period. (See Nina Youngstrom, "Malpractice Premiums Jump 50 Percent Aug. 1," *APA Monitor*, August 1990, p. 16.) There are approximately 353,000 members of the clergy in the United States; this figure does not include nonclergy professionals or lay Christian counselors. (See Constant H. Jacquet, ed., *Yearbook of American and Canadian Churches* [Nashville: Abingdon, 1990], p. 255.) As trends toward litigation continue to increase, the potential for such lawsuits could have staggering effects on Christian churches and ministries.
2. Nally v. Grace Community Church of the Valley, 763 P.2d 948 (S.Ct. Cal. 1988).

while a student at UCLA in 1974 he began attending the Grace Community Church of the Valley, pastored by John MacArthur.

Southern California is a land of "super-churches" (commonly defined as churches with more than 10,000 members) and superstar pastors, including Calvary Chapel (Chuck Smith), The Crystal Cathedral (Robert Schuller), and the First Evangelical Free Church of Fullerton (Chuck Swindoll). One of the largest churches in Southern California is the Grace Community Church in Sun Valley. Its pastor, John MacArthur, a well-known author and educator, is known as a solid, conservative Bible teacher.

When a person leaves one church or denomination for another, there are often hard feelings with family and friends. Ken Nally was no exception. His "conversion" to evangelicalism became a source of friction between him and his family. To complicate things further, Ken had been depressed since the previous year over a breakup with his girlfriend.

In 1975, Ken began seeing a secular psychologist to discuss problems he was having with his girlfriend. After his graduation from UCLA the following year, he enrolled for one semester in Talbot Theological Seminary's extension campus at the Grace Community Church. During this time he became involved with another girlfriend, who was a fellow Talbot student, beginning a relationship that would eventually break up in December 1978.

Earlier in 1978, Ken began a "discipling relationship" with one of the pastors at Grace Community Church, meeting with the pastor five times before losing interest. Prior to 1979, these five meetings constituted the full extent of Ken's counseling relationship with the church.

Following the breakup with his girlfriend, Ken became increasingly despondent. In February 1979, Ken's mother arranged for him to see a Dr. Milestone, a general practitioner, who prescribed Elavil to relieve his depression. Later the same month, Ken saw another physician who suggested that he undergo a full physical examination. Neither physician recommended that he see a psychiatrist.

Shortly thereafter, Ken went to a drop-in counseling session with another of the pastors at Grace Community Church, where he spoke briefly about the marital tensions between his parents and the problems he was having with his new, current girlfriend.

The following month, Ken attempted suicide by taking an overdose of the Elavil that had been prescribed by Dr. Milestone. His parents found him and took him to the hospital, where a Dr. Evelyn, the attending physician, advised the parents that, because Ken "was actually suicidal," she could not authorize his release from the hospital until he had seen a psychiatrist. Four days later, a staff psychiatrist, Dr. Hall, examined Ken and recommended that he commit himself to a psychiatric hospital. Ken refused and was discharged from the hospital.

Upon his release, Ken stayed with Pastor MacArthur because he did not want to return home. MacArthur encouraged him to keep his appointments with Dr. Hall, the psychiatrist, and arranged for Ken to be examined by Dr. John Parker, a physician and church deacon. Parker's examination indicated that Ken was still suicidal, and he too recommended that Ken commit himself for psychiatric treatment. Again Ken refused.

Parker then spoke with Ken's parents and offered to arrange for his involuntary commitment, but the parents rejected the offer. A week before his suicide, Ken moved back home and, during the final week of his life, was examined separately by two more physicians who agreed that he needed further physical and psychiatric evaluation.

Later that week, Ken saw a psychologist and a registered psychologist's assistant. A few days later, he was found dead in a friend's apartment, the victim of a self-inflicted gunshot wound.

## The Outcome of the *Nally* Case

The record shows that, in the two-month period between February 1979 and his death, Ken saw at least four physicians, one psychiatrist, a psychologist, and a psychologist's assistant and had several counseling sessions with pastors at

Grace Community Church. Walter and Maria Nally, Ken's parents, could have sued anyone who had seen their son over the few months prior to his death, but they chose the Grace Community Church of the Valley. They charged, among other things, wrongful death based on "clergyman malpractice," negligent counseling, and even "outrageous conduct for teaching certain Protestant religious doctrines that conflicted with Nally's Catholic upbringing."[3] They alleged that following his suicide attempt by Elavil overdose, the pastors "actively and affirmatively dissuaded and discouraged [Ken] from seeking further psychological and/or psychiatric care."[4]

Despite the record showing that the pastors encouraged Ken to keep his appointments with physicians and outside counseling professionals, the case went through the California court system twice before the Supreme Court of California exonerated the church in November 1988. The bottom line is that after two victories at the trial court level and two losses at the appeal court level, the Grace Community Church of the Valley won the case in the state Supreme Court. However, the case was in litigation for more than nine years, and a fortune in legal fees was expended in defending the right to engage in a counseling ministry without fear of reprisal.

## The Impact of the *Nally* Decision

The key question in the *Nally* case was whether the pastors, as spiritual counselors, had a duty to refer Ken Nally to professional secular counselors who were in a position to help prevent his suicide. The Court of Appeal ruled that "nontherapist [nonlicensed] counselors—*both religious and secular*—have a duty to refer suicidal persons to psychiatrists or psychotherapists qualified to prevent suicides."[5]

In reversing the Court of Appeal, the state Supreme Court rejected the imposition of a broad "duty to refer," not only for the defendants, but for nontherapist counselors in

3. Ibid. at 952.
4. Ibid.
5. Ibid. at 954 (italics original).

general.[6] Addressing pastoral counselors specifically, the court stated:

> The legislature has exempted the clergy from the licensing requirements applicable to marriage, family, child and domestic counselors and from the operation of statutes regulating psychologists. In so doing, the Legislature has recognized that access to the clergy should be free from state imposed counseling standards, and that "the secular state is not equipped to ascertain the competence of counseling when performed by those affiliated with religious organizations."[7]

Expanding their holding to nontherapist counselors in general, the court noted:

> Generally, there is a real question about the closeness of the causal connection between a nontherapist counselor's failure to refer to professional help and the suicide of a particular suicidal person. By their very definition, nontherapist counselors are not professional medical experts on suicide. Their activities are undertaken pursuant to doctrines explicitly left unregulated by the state.[8]

The *Nally* holding is a "good news–bad news" decision. The good news is that, in addition to religious counselors, the decision protects peer counselors, self-help groups (such as alcoholism or cancer support groups), crisis hotlines (e.g., teenage drug abuse or suicide prevention hotlines), and nonprofessional sexual abuse counselors (e.g., Women Organized Against Rape).

The bad news is that, while it protects Christians who are competent to counsel, it leaves counseling unregulated to the extent that there will be Christians who are *not* competent to counsel and acting without accountability to a local church or legitimate counseling agency. This, however, is a trade-off, since by nature the regulation of Christian counselors should come through churches rather than through the

6. Ibid.
7. Ibid. at 959-60.
8. Ibid. at 958-59, fn. 7.

state. In short, charlatans will still be allowed to practice. However, allowing this may be a "necessary evil" in light of the constitutional protection available to *legitimate* religious counselors.

## Did We Really Win the War?

The *Nally* case went through the California court system twice. The Superior Court of Los Angeles held that the Nallys did not have a sufficient case to litigate against the church, but the Court of Appeal found the church to be negligent. The state Supreme Court denied review and remanded the case back to the Superior Court, which again found no cause for action. The case then went back to the Appeal Court, which again reversed and held the church liable. Finally, the California Supreme Court heard the case and issued a final decision in 1988. The Nallys then appealed the case to the United States Supreme Court, which denied certiorari (refused to hear the case, thus allowing the California Supreme Court opinion to stand).

A side observation is appropriate here. If the Nallys had sued a church *other* than the Grace Community Church, the result may not have been the same. As a large fellowship on solid financial ground, having a dedicated pastoral staff and access to good legal resources, the church was able to carry its court appeals through to the state Supreme Court level. Had they been a "small country church" with less resources, the case would likely not have gone past the appeal court level, and the Nallys would have won.

If we look at each of the trials as a battle, it would be easy to say that the Grace Community Church lost a few battles but won the war. But it's not that simple. I believe that the entire *Nally* case can be looked at as one battle and that the war over whether Christian counselors should be regulated by secular authorities or be liable in secular courts will continue to rage in other courts and in other states. It is, I'm afraid, a legal war that the church may not win.

I make that statement carefully. The expression "I read the end of the Book, and we win" is certainly true in terms of ultimate victory from a theological perspective. However, there will be more legal battles ahead as other malpractice suits are filed against churches, pastors, and Christian counseling professionals. Even if those suits are unsuccessful for the plaintiffs, the legal expenses incurred by churches and counseling ministries will take their toll on the effectiveness of the work (not to mention time and energy expended in trial preparation and court proceedings).

In the age of litigation, Christian counselors forced to defend themselves in the secular court system are "sheep in the midst of wolves" and must be "as shrewd as serpents, and innocent as doves" (Matthew 10:16). As the next chapter illustrates, the battles continue. Yet a knowledge of how the law impacts Christian counselors will aid counselors to "fight the good fight of faith" (1 Timothy 6:12) in the secular arena.

# 2

# An Explosive New Area of Law

In May of 1989, a group of attorneys gathered in San Francisco for a seminar sponsored by the American Bar Association (ABA) called *Tort and Religion.* Sponsored by the Section of Tort and Insurance Practice, Section of Individual Rights and Responsibilities of the ABA's Division for Professional Education, the seminar was touted for "attorneys who want to be on the leading edge of an explosive new area of law."[1] The purpose of the seminar was, in effect, to train attorneys in how to sue churches. For many of them, it was the first time they were exposed to any element of law with regard to its impact on religion.

## The Making of a Modern Attorney

To understand the dilemma that pastors and Christian counselors face with regard to the legal status of their work, it may help to examine the differences between legal and theological education today.

Religious education, for the most part, is unregulated by federal or state government agencies. Some churches or denominations maintain a minimum standard for the granting of

1. Brochure for the American Bar Association's *Tort and Religion* seminar, May 4-5, 1989, San Francisco, Calif. Quoted in J. Shelby Sharpe, "The Coming Nuclear Attack on Christianity in America: A Report on the American Bar Association Seminar *Tort and Religion*" (Fort Worth, Tex.: Sharpe, Bates & McGee, 1989), p. 1.

pastoral credentials, such as a Master of Divinity (M.Div.) degree from an accredited seminary, while others train their pastors within the church and require neither a college nor seminary degree. Likewise, credentials for lay or professional Christian counselors vary, with requirements ranging from no formal education to a graduate degree, such as an M.A. in counseling.

Legal education, on the other hand, is regulated both by the government and by professional associations. In forty-three states and the District of Columbia, a person must graduate from a law school approved by the American Bar Association to be eligible to sit for the state bar.

The M.Div. degree, often referred to as the first professional degree for a pastor, varies little between American seminaries and has a small number of elective credit hours available. The program is highly scoped and is designed to provide a pastor with a solid background in various areas of pastoral concern, including biblical and systematic theology, hermeneutics and homiletics, biblical languages, counseling, and practical theology.

The law school curriculum proscribed by the American Bar Association and by various state bars consists of the same number of academic credits as the average M.Div. degree. Unlike the M.Div. curriculum at most seminaries, however, which is designed to include a wide range of theological subject areas, only one-third of the average Juris Doctorate, or professional law curriculum, consists of required courses; the remainder are elective in nature.[2]

2. It is interesting to note that for an equal amount of credit hours applied to their respective "first professional degrees," pastors earn the Master of Divinity while lawyers earn the Juris Doctorate (J.D.). Until the early 1960s, the most common law degree was the Bachelor of Laws (LL.B.). But many attorneys felt that, since physicians and other professionals received a doctorate degree for their three or more years of graduate study, lawyers deserved more than a second bachelor's degree. American law schools universally agreed and changed their first professional degree from the LL.B. to the J.D. Many schools offered their alumni the opportunity to convert their LL.B. diplomas into Juris Doctorates, and a large percentage accepted. Today the LL.B. is reserved for those law schools that admit students who have not earned a bachelor's degree but have at least 60 semester hours of undergraduate credit. Those who graduate law school and have a previously earned bachelor's degree are granted the J.D., while those who graduate law school without a previously earned degree are granted the LL.B. The graduate

Most law schools require only one semester of study in constitutional law, the course area in which the relationship between religion and law is normally taught. (Some law schools don't require constitutional law at all.) However, freedom of religion issues are usually not covered until the *second* semester of constitutional law, and then only in the course of one three-hour lecture and one chapter in the students' constitutional law textbook.

The result is that most attorneys in practice today have received *no* training in the adjudication of religious cases. While they may be competent in their respective specializations (e.g., corporate law, taxation, family law, litigation, criminal law), there are few lawyers who are adept at entering a courtroom to defend a religious cause. According to a partner in a prominent Philadelphia law firm,

> the danger is that the law is so complicated today. . . . The areas of law are as different one from another as the specialties of medicine. You wouldn't expect a psychiatrist to perform reconstructive surgery on your knee. But that's what some lawyers do, lawyers who desperately want to hold on to any business that walks in their door. They somehow have the notion that because they have a law degree, and because all a lawyer does is work with words, they can handle anything. God help their clients.[3]

Attorneys who handle religious cases and do their job well, albeit without law school training in this area, end up having to spend significant time on legal research. This time is then billed to the client—the church.

law degree is the LL.M., or Master of Laws. Therefore, unlike in theology, in which the student earns one or more masters degrees (e.g., M.A., M.Div., S.T.M., Th.M.) and then a doctorate (e.g., a D.Min., Th.D., or Ph.D.), the attorney usually earns the doctorate as his or her first professional degree, then a masters as the terminal credential.

3. Art Carey, "The United States of Incompetence," *The Philadelphia Inquirer Magazine*, 25 February 1989, p. 18.

## The Dilemma Today

Enter the American Bar Association, which has apparently decided that it is more appropriate to train attorneys in how to *sue* churches than in how to *defend* them. It would be easy to assume that the influence at work in the ABA is satanic or philosophically anti-Christian. Surveys indicate that people who have been through a bad legal experience generally hold a poor image of lawyers, and the phrase "Christian lawyer" has been termed an oxymoron[4] by both lay people and attorneys.

While I agree with many theologians that Satan is at work in the world today, I lean toward the view that the sudden interest on the part of the ABA in suing churches is primarily the recognition of a new "deep pocket" that will result in financial gain. In short, it's not that the ABA is operating from an anti-Christian moral base; rather, they are operating from no moral base at all and are looking to the potential financial awards they can win in this "explosive new area of law."

The most popular courses in the average ABA-approved law school include civil law, commercial law, corporate law, criminal law, environmental and health law, labor law, litigation, property and probate, taxation, and tort law. The reason is simple: these areas result in more lucrative careers for lawyers than constitutional law and church-state issues. The lack of lawyers competently trained in how to defend churches shouldn't be surprising; the church-state arena isn't perceived to be a profitable area of law by attorneys themselves.

Because of the perceived financial rewards in suing churches, however, attorneys are learning how to work *against* churches. The ABA's San Francisco seminar included, among other workshops, the following presentations:

4. An oxymoron is a combination of seemingly contradictory or incongruous words that form a common expression, such as *burning cold, sweet sorrow, military intelligence,* or in this case, *Christian lawyer.*

- Expanding Use of Tort Law Against Religions
- Tort Law as an Ideological Weapon
- Tort Law as Essential Restraint on Religious Abuses
- Liability of Clergy as Spiritual Counselors
- Tort Liability for Fraud, Emotional Distress and Harm to Reputation Arising from Religiously Motivated Conduct
- Tort Liability for Brainwashing
- Liability for Sexual Conduct of the Clergy
- Institutional Liability for Negligent Hiring/Retention
- Piercing the Corporate Veil: Liability of Religious Bodies and Affiliated Entities[5]

A second ABA conference on Tort and Religion was held in Boston in June 1990 and was somewhat more balanced in terms of presenting lectures on how to defend churches as well as how to sue them.[6] Nonetheless, the mere presentation of such conferences significantly increases the chances that churches *will* be sued.

A solution to this dilemma is for pastors and Christian counselors to learn the law themselves. One way this is being accomplished is through the inclusion of legal study in Bible colleges and seminaries as a form of "preventive medicine." Instruction in how the law impacts the church and the development of law courses geared specifically to pastors, parachurch workers, and Christian counselors may be likened to a health maintenance organization in which *preventive medicine* can be practiced so *corrective litigation* will not be necessary. The inclusion of legal education in the theological curriculum also ensures that each of the above areas can be treated from an ethical as well as a legal perspective, examining both the *is* and the *ought*, and that the biblical ramifications of the law can be included as part of the educational program.

5. Sharpe, pp. 2-3.
6. For a summary and review of the Boston conference, see Richard R. Hammar, "Tort and Religion—The American Bar Association Conference on Church Litigation," *Church Law & Tax Report*, July-August 1990, pp. 2-5.

The Bible reflects the stand that the church will survive with or without legal education in theological learning. Yet as litigation against churches increases in the next few years, the addition of training in law as it affects the church will provide an extra coat of armor that will help churches and ministries function in such a way that they'll be able to withstand increasing legal attack.

## THE MYTH OF CLERGY MALPRACTICE

Much of the concern over the legal ramifications of counseling and other areas of the pastoral ministry centers on the concept of clergy malpractice. There's good news and bad news to report with regard to clergy malpractice as a tort claim. The good news is that functionally, there's no such thing. The bad news is that any number of other tort claims exist for which clergy can be held responsible.

Looking at another profession may help illustrate the situation. Assume, for example, that you own a house and one day your water pipes burst. You call a plumber, he comes to your house, fixes your water pipes, and rapes you (or your spouse). The bad news, for the plumber, is that he will be charged (and hopefully convicted) of the crime of rape. What he will *not* be charged with is "plumber malpractice."

Criminal charges aside, you and/or your spouse may sue the plumber for, among other things, outrageous conduct, intentional infliction of emotional distress, and alienation of affection. The likelihood is that you may win on any or all of these tort claims. On the other hand, you're not likely to sue him for plumber malpractice, and it's highly improbable that you would win such a claim anyway.

The situation is the same with regard to inappropriate actions by members of the clergy. In *DeStefano v. Grabrian*,[7] for example, a Catholic priest who had been acting as a marriage counselor became sexually involved with the female spouse in the marriage, contributing to the couple's ultimate divorce. The husband sued both his ex-wife and the priest;

7. DeStefano v. Grabian, 763 P.2d 275 (S.Ct. Colo. 1988).

later, the husband dismissed the claims against his ex-wife, and she joined the suit against the priest and the diocese. Reversing lower courts, the Supreme Court of Colorado upheld the couple's right to sue the priest for breach of a fiduciary relationship and outrageous conduct, as well as to sue the diocese for negligent supervision.

In *Hester v. Barnett,*[8] a pastor began a counseling relationship with a couple that was having disciplinary problems with their children. Despite assuring them that any communication with him as a minister would be kept in strict confidence, the pastor proceeded to spread false rumors among the congregation that the Hesters were thieves and scoundrels who beat, whipped, and otherwise abused their children. Although the pastor later apologized to the Hesters for his conduct and prayed for forgiveness in their presence, he continued to spread rumors about them and would not retract his statements in public. The court held that the pastor could be sued for alienation of affections, defamation of character, intentional infliction of emotional distress, invasion of privacy, and interference with contract.[9]

In *St. Luke Evangelical Lutheran Church v. Smith,*[10] a pastor accused one of his copastors and a church secretary of having an affair. Rather than approaching the parties directly, the pastor made the allegations to several relatives of the parties and other members of the congregation, resulting in the secretary's dismissal. She sued the pastor and the church and was awarded a judgment of almost $337,000. Both the pastor and the church (as the pastor's employer) were found guilty of defamation of character and invasion of privacy.

In *Erickson v. Christenson,*[11] the Oregon Court of Appeals held that a woman who had been seduced by her pastor at age thirteen, resulting in an affair that lasted several years, had the right to sue both the pastor, his church, and the

8. Hester v. Barnett, 723 S.W.2d 544 (Mo. App. 1987).
9. The claim of interference with contract resulted from the pastor's alleged harassment and intimidation of employees who worked for the Hesters in their farming business, resulting in their leaving the Hesters' employment.
10. St. Luke Evangelical Church v. Smith, 568 A.2d 35 (S.Ct. Md. 1990).
11. Erickson v. Christenson, 781 P.2d 383 (Or. App. 1989).

church's parent denomination for intentional infliction of emotional harm, church liability for the torts of the pastor, and negligent supervision.

In each of the above cases, the courts held that the pastors could not be sued for the tort of clergy malpractice, primarily due to the fact that the tort had not been established in any jurisdiction in which the cases were heard. The courts also held that the claims in these cases were not barred on the basis of First Amendment grounds that would prohibit litigation based on impermissible government interference with clergy or church conduct. Since other claims existed, the questionable tort of clergy malpractice per se did not even have to be addressed. According to the Supreme Court of Ohio,

> malpractice, it must be noted, is not a theory of ordinary negligence or of intentional tort. It is a separate and distinct course of action. A tortfeasor [the party being sued] may be liable for acts of ordinary negligence or for intentional torts, regardless of the "professional" color of his conduct.
>
> For clergy malpractice to be recognized, the cleric's behavior, even if it is related to his "professional" duties, must fall outside the scope of other recognized torts.[12]

The fact that clergy malpractice is not a recognized tort claim should not lull pastors or churches into a false sense of security. Though the plumber who rapes a customer cannot be sued for plumber malpractice, there are many other claims that will hold up in court against him. Though, at this point, pastors who commit negligent acts cannot be sued for clergy malpractice, there are likewise many claims for which they can be sued successfully.

A final caveat is appropriate here. Lawsuits against pastors or counselors who *intentionally* commit actionable torts may, in fact, be justified. Most commonly, suits against pastors and Christian counselors generally result from acts of seduction, child abuse, and defamation. It would be ideal if pastors, counselors, and other Christians never engaged in

12. Strock v. Pressnell, 527 N.E.2d 1235, 1239 (S.Ct. Ohio 1988).

such actions. However, human nature is such that even Christian professionals will fail to maintain the moral standards the Word of God has set for them.

At the same time, lawsuits against pastors and counselors who have breached appropriate moral and professional standards will reflect negatively upon pastors and counselors who do maintain such standards in their practice. Justified lawsuits have resulted in a domino effect, in which churches and counselors will be sued even when a legitimate cause of action does not exist.

For Christian counselors, then, there must be a continuous emphasis on maintaining standards that will help ensure the avoidance of legal action. For scriptural as well as for legal reasons, the object should not be to avoid getting caught for committing tortious actions but to avoid committing such actions at all.

# 3

# The First Freedom

The differences between Christian counseling and secular counseling from a methodological perspective are obvious. Christian counseling accepts the Bible as both a moral base and an absolute standard for faith and conduct; secular counseling believes that people are autonomous and that the standards for faith and conduct are relative and experiential. Christian counseling integrates prayer, Scripture, and a reliance on the leading of the Holy Spirit in an individual's life; secular counseling advises a person to "do your own thing" without regard to a higher authority. Secular counseling's support systems include psychiatry, psychology, psychoanalysis, biofeedback, meditation, and medication; the primary support systems in Christian counseling are the Holy Spirit, the Word of God, and accountability to other believers.[1]

Legally, Christian counseling falls under the general term *spiritual*, or *religious*, counseling and enters a realm that civil courts are neither prepared nor permitted to adjudicate from a doctrinal perspective. In terms of the law, the primary difference between spiritual and secular counseling is in the area of regulation. While secular counseling can be regulated by the government, a regulatory agency, or a licensing board, spiritual counseling deals with religious beliefs, and

1. An interesting study in mutual Christian accountability is to reference the phrase "one another" in a comprehensive concordance. To do so provides an ideal introduction to one of the primary support systems recommended in Christian counseling.

courts are precluded from making value judgments as to the truth or falsehood of those beliefs.

The freedom to subscribe to the religious faith of one's choice (or not to subscribe to any religious belief system at all) is based on the First Amendment to the United States Constitution:

> Congress shall make no law respecting an establishment of religion, or prohibiting the free exercise thereof; or abridging the freedom of speech, or of the press; or the right of the people peaceably to assemble, and to petition the Government for a redress of grievances.[2]

Because religion is mentioned first in the Bill of Rights, it has become known as "the first freedom." Consisting of two clauses, this part of the First Amendment signifies that (1) the government cannot prefer one religion over another (known as the Establishment clause), and (2) the government cannot prohibit the free exercise of a person's chosen faith (known as the Free Exercise clause).

In terms of religious practice, the Free Exercise clause has been interpreted by the courts to mean that there can be no interference whatsoever with a person's right to *believe* what he or she chooses in terms of religion. There may, however, be restrictions placed upon *action* based on a person's belief. In the late 1800s, for example, the Mormon Church practiced polygamy as a sincerely held religious belief. The Supreme Court ruled, however, that while they had the right to *believe* in polygamy, they did not have the right to *practice* plural marriage. Using the *argumentum ad horrendum* to uphold the conviction of a polygamous Mormon, the court noted that if they were to allow the practice of polygamy based on religious belief, the ruling might be used to justify human sacrifice as a religious practice or a wife's burning herself to death on her husband's funeral pyre as a religious duty.[3] The same doctrine has also been used in health-related issues, ex-

2. U.S. Constitution, amend. I.
3. Reynolds v. United States, 98 U.S. 145 (1878).

amples being when Christian Scientists or Jehovah's Witnesses refuse medical care or blood transfusions for their children.

This "action-belief dichotomy" has been expanded to form the doctrine of "sincerely held religious belief." While courts today may adjudicate a case based on whether a person sincerely believes what he or she purports to believe, the court may not determine whether the beliefs held are true or false.[4]

In terms of counseling, the courts' practice of not adjudicating the truth claims of religious beliefs has provided a freedom for Christian counselors (and other religiously based counselors) that secular counseling does not enjoy. Much of this is due to the *Lemon* test, established by the Supreme Court in 1971. Based on the case of *Lemon v. Kurtzman*,[5] the Court held that in forming statutes dealing with religion, (1) the statute must have a primary secular purpose, (2) the statute must neither advance nor inhibit religion, and (3) the statute must not foster excessive government entanglement with religion. In addition to legislation, the *Lemon* test applies to policies, procedures, regulations, or any other government action touching on religious matters. The result is that spiritual counseling is less open to judicial scrutiny in a lawsuit than secular counseling.

The question we must ask, then, is, What makes any given counseling issue religious rather than secular? Take, for example, issues such as marriage and the family, abortion, sexuality, addiction, and depression. What, if anything, makes these issues religious? What makes them secular?

4. A good example of this principle is provided in the case of *United States v. Ballard* (322 U.S. 78 [1944]). Guy and Edna Ballard, founders of the "I Am" movement, were convicted of fraud after using the mails to represent that they could heal diseases and other ailments or injuries by virtue of supernatural powers. The U.S. Supreme Court affirmed the district court judge's admonition to the jury not to consider whether the Ballards' claims were true but simply whether the Ballards *believed* them to be true. In part, the Court based its opinion on the ruling of *Watson v. Jones* (80 U.S. [13 Wall.] 679 [1872]), an early church property dispute case that set the following precedent: "The law knows no heresy, and is committed to the support of no dogma, the establishment of no sect." Today, therefore, cases involving religious issues will generally be ruled upon based on neutral principles of law and whether religious beliefs are sincerely held, rather than on the truth claims of the actual religious beliefs.
5. Lemon v. Kurtzman, 403 U.S. 602 (1971).

More to the point, what makes the religious counselor more or less qualified to deal with these issues than the secular counselor?

I wish I could provide an easy answer, but in terms of the court system, there is none. The average secular counselor will say that the basic key to marriage and family counseling is interpersonal relationships; the average Christian counselor will say that the solution to a marriage or family problem can best be found in the Word of God. The problem with these arguments is that the courts are precluded from making a value judgment that Christians have no problem making.

When counselors invoke religious principles in their defense, a key question that must be addressed by the courts is whether disputed conduct is religious or secular. While the root cause of a strained marital relationship may not be thought of as a religious issue by a secular counselor, the Christian counselor views the cause of the problem as spiritual in nature. This illustrates the conflict between secular and Christian counseling: an intrinsic difference in worldview results in animosity between the two camps.

## The Worldview Factor

One of the issues in the *Nally* case was the allegation that the pastors at Grace Community Church of the Valley prevented Kenneth Nally from seeing secular counseling professionals. This is disproved by the court records, which indicate that the pastors encouraged Ken to keep his appointments with physicians and psychologists.

There are, however, legitimate instances where it would be inappropriate to refer a counseling client or parishioner to a secular counselor, and this is based upon the basic conflict between Christian and secular counselors with regard to spiritual values.

At the same time, many secular counselors are antagonistic toward the Christian faith and are unwilling to work within a Christian counseling framework. The conflict, in short, is mutual. Secular counselors tend not to refer clients to pastors, and vice versa.

One study has indicated that only 43 percent of psychiatrists and as little as 5 percent of the membership of the American Psychological Association profess a belief in God.[6] The survey does not indicate, however, whether the phrase "belief in God" necessarily connotes a Christian framework.

The bottom line is that secular counselors tend to blame their clients' problems on their Christian faith, while Christian counselors have a legitimate concern that secular counselors will attempt to pull the client away from Christianity. Therefore, there is little cooperation between secular and Bible-believing counselors. This, of course, does not answer the basic question: Who is more qualified to treat the problems enumerated in this chapter? And who shall be the arbiter of determining such qualifications?

Walter and Maria Nally appeared to feel that secular counselors would have been more competent in treating Ken Nally's depression. The pastors at Grace Community Church, while they cooperated with secular professionals, likely felt that they were just as competent as any secular counselor. In short, the determination of competence is subjective in nature: non-Christians will feel that secular counselors are better equipped to deal with emotional problems, while Christians will feel that the ultimate answers to such problems are in Scripture. The bad news is that even Christians sitting on the judicial bench are not in a position to uphold Scripture based on its inherent truth. The good news is that, because the courts cannot adjudicate a case based on the truth inherent in Christianity's claims, Christian counselors are free to practice more freely than their secular counterparts.

## COMPELLING STATE INTEREST

The freedom of Christian counselors to practice is, however, open to scrutiny based on the doctrine of compelling state interest. Developed in the cases of *Sherbert v. Verner*[7]

6. David B. Larson et al., "Systematic Analysis of Research on Religious Variables in Four Major Psychiatric Journals, 1978-1982," *American Journal of Psychiatry* 143 (March 1986): 329.
7. Sherbert v. Verner, 374 U.S. 398 (1963).

and *Wisconsin v. Yoder,*[8] the Supreme Court has determined that, for a state regulation to interfere with the free exercise of a person's religious belief, three questions must be asked. First, is the activity in question motivated and rooted in a legitimately and sincerely held religious belief? Second, is the right to free exercise of religion being unduly burdened by the state regulation and, if so, what is the extent of its impact on religious practice? Finally, does the state have a sufficiently compelling interest in the regulation to justify the burden on the free exercise of religion?

In the *Sherbert* case, the Court held that the state did not have a sufficiently compelling interest to withhold unemployment benefits from Adele Sherbert, a Seventh Day Adventist who was fired from her job for refusing to work on her Saturday Sabbath. In *Yoder*, the Court ruled that the state of Wisconsin did not have a sufficiently compelling interest to prohibit Old Order Amish parents from removing their children from the public school system after the eighth grade.

On the other hand, in early 1990 the Court appeared to move away from traditional interpretations of the doctrine when they ruled in *Employment Division, Oregon Department of Human Resources v. Smith*[9] that the state had a suf-

8. Wisconsin v. Yoder, 406 U.S. 205 (1972).
9. Employment Division, Oregon Department of Human Resources v. Smith, 110 S.Ct. 4433 (1990). While a compelling state interest was demonstrated in this case, there is a consensus in legal thinking that *Smith* may begin a trend in which compelling state interest is no longer considered the predominant doctrine in the adjudication of religious cases. In the majority opinion, Justice Antonin Scalia held that for a religious right to be protected, it must be integrated with another constitutional right (e.g., the issue could involve both freedom of religion and freedom of speech). By itself, Scalia held, freedom of religion did not demand special consideration if a law is content-neutral on its face, i.e., if it affects all persons equally without regard to religion. Thus, if the burden of a law on a person's religious freedom is incidental, that is simply a price to be paid. The ruling has been viewed by legal scholars as potentially damaging to religious freedoms.

   A concurring opinion by Justice Sandra Day O'Connor also held that there is no constitutional right to use drugs in the context of religious ceremonies. However, O'Connor based her opinion on the traditional compelling state interest argument in *Sherbert* and *Yoder.* An interesting side note is that the Court's liberal justices (Blackmun, Brennan, Marshall), while feeling that the state did not have a compelling interest in forbidding Native Americans to use peyote, held that Justice Scalia's majority opinion had the potential of overturning established law regarding religious rights.

ficiently compelling interest—the prevention of drug abuse—in refusing members of the Native American Church the right to use peyote in their religious services.

How might the compelling state interest doctrine work in terms of Christian counseling? Take the hypothetical case of John Smith, a pastor with an active counseling ministry. Pastor John believes in the literal interpretation of the Word of God and has a sincerely held religious belief that Christians should go to be with the Lord at their earliest opportunity. It seems that Pastor John, who doesn't devote much attention to hermeneutics, has his own way of interpreting Paul's words in Philippians, which appear as follows:

> For to me, to live is Christ, and to die is gain. But if I am to live on in the flesh, this will mean fruitful labor for me; and I do not know which to choose. But I am hard-pressed from both directions, having the desire to depart and be with Christ, for that is very much better. (Philippians 1:21-23)

As Pastor John's parishioners come to him for counseling, they exhibit signs of depression, failing health, poor relationships, and an inability to cope with life's problems. So Pastor John counsels them to the effect that to die is gain—they will go to be with Christ, and their problems will cease.

It is no wonder that Pastor John has a high suicide rate in his congregation. It shouldn't be surprising that one or more family members of his dead parishioners will sue him—and his church—for, among other things, outrageous conduct, negligence, malpractice, intentional infliction of emotional distress, and any other torts their attorneys can think of. It would also be logical to assume that the state may bring criminal charges against Pastor John for his actions (one might recollect the actions of Jim Jones and the People's Temple at this point).

For background on the potential ramifications of the case for Christians, see "The Death of Liberty?" *The Briefcase* (newsletter of the Christian Law Association), July 1990, pp. 1, 6.

Here is a situation in which the state obviously has a sufficiently compelling interest (the basic preservation of life) to regulate the activities of a spiritual counselor. Why didn't this provide a compelling state interest in the *Nally* case that would have caused the California Supreme Court to rule against the Grace Community Church? There was such an interest. But in *Nally* the court recognized that the pastoral counselors at Grace Community Church acted responsibly in their relationship with Ken Nally and met any duty of care they might have had by referring him to other professionals.

However, in *Nally* the court held that pastoral counselors do *not* have a duty of care. The ruling would likely have been different if the pastors had not acted responsibly. In fact, in a concurring opinion, one judge noted that, while he agreed with the outcome of the case with regard to the Grace Community Church, he felt that the church *did* owe Ken Nally a duty of care.[10]

## IMPOSING A DUTY OF CARE

The First Amendment, then, ensures that Christian counselors, to the extent that they are acting in a responsible manner, are protected in terms of the spiritual content of their counseling. Yet an increasing number of legal scholars agree that a duty of care will be (and some feel, should be) imposed upon spiritual counselors, especially clergy, in future cases:

> Clergy counselors should be subject to liability for negligent counseling. They also should be licensed to ensure their competence. Neither the imposition of a duty of care nor a licensing requirement would violate the first amendment. Furthermore, public policy and recognized tort doctrines support establishing a minimally burdensome duty of care and a licensing requirement.
>
> Courts should require that clergy counselors who hold themselves out as competent to deal with serious emotional illness be capable of understanding basic psychological prob-

10. Nally, 763 P.2d at 964 (Justice Kaufman, concurring).

> lems. Clergy counselors should also be able to identify these troubles in their counselees and recognize when they, as counselors, are no longer competent to treat those counselees. Once clergy counselors have identified a counselee's problem and found it beyond their level of competence, courts should require them to refer that counselee to a professional therapist. This duty to refer would require clergy counselors only to try to persuade—not to force—a counselee to contact a professional therapist for treatment. Such a duty of care would be a minimal burden for clergy counselors.[11]

The problem with imposing such a duty is that it would be difficult to establish standards that can be applied to all religions equally. Keep in mind that, although Christian counselors will commonly agree that Christianity is the only legitimate truth system in terms of religious thinking, the American law system is designed to protect any and all religious beliefs, no matter how popular, unpopular, or false. Even the *Nally* court recognized this:

> Because of the differing theological views espoused by the myriad of religions in our state and practiced by church members, it would certainly be impractical, and quite possibly unconstitutional, to impose a duty of care on pastoral counselors. Such a duty would necessarily be intertwined with the religious philosophy of the particular denomination or ecclesiastical teachings of the religious entity.[12]

Taking this logic outside the Judeo-Christian realm, Terry Wuester Milne writes:

> Because of varying beliefs and counseling practices of American clergy, no single standard exists which could be applicable to all clergy. What is promulgated by one faith may be completely unreasonable in another. No licensing requirements or recognized voluntary associations exist which encompass

11. Robert C. Troyer, "Protecting the Flock from the Shepherd: A Duty of Care and Licensing Requirement for Clergy Counselors," *Boston College Law Review* 30 (1989): 1207.
12. Nally, 763 P.2d at 960.

> even the majority of clergypersons in the United States. Even if one could articulate standards which might be applicable to Judeo-Christian religious leaders, this standard would likely be inapplicable to persons such as Christian Science practitioners, self-proclaimed gurus, and other leaders who hold beliefs outside the mainstream of American religion.[13]

The courts, and possibly legislative bodies, may feel they are forced at some point to examine the feasibility of professional standards for spiritual counselors. When they do, however, "Standardization of training will undoubtedly be attacked as a violation of the free exercise clause by the various sects which hold religious beliefs that are incompatible with such training."[14]

In the meantime, the best course of action for Christian counselors is to realize that constitutional protection is not absolute and that, although the courts may not yet hold counselors to a duty of care toward the parishioner or client, it is best to act as if there is such a duty. Certainly, even though the law may not recognize a duty of care, the Lord admonishes us to exercise such a duty and to "be full of goodness, filled with all knowledge, and able to admonish one another" (Romans 15:14).

13. Terry Wuester Milne, "Bless Me, Father, for I Am About to Sin . . . Should Clergy Counselors Have a Duty to Protect Third Parties?" *Tulsa Law Journal* 22 (1986): 162-63.
14. Robert J. Basil, "Clergy Malpractice: Taking Spiritual Counseling Conflicts Beyond Intentional Tort Analysis," *Rutgers Law Journal* 19 (1988): 444-45.

# 4

# What Makes a Counselor a Counselor?

In determining the degree to which a person may be held liable under the law in the realm of counseling, it is important to define the various roles and capacities in which a person may serve as a Christian counselor. To some degree, every Christian is called upon to counsel other Christians. The apostle James tells us, "My brethren, if any among you strays from the truth, and one turns him back; let him know that he who turns a sinner from the error of his way will save his soul from death, and will cover a multitude of sins" (James 5:19-20). Counseling is not limited to pastors or professionals; we are all exhorted to "encourage one another, and build up one another" (1 Thessalonians 5:11) and to "confess your sins to one another, and pray for one another, so that you may be healed" (James 5:16).

At the same time, God has also raised up persons to be professional counselors, devoting their full-time work to the ministry of counseling. In his last pastoral letter, Paul wrote to Timothy, "Preach the word; be ready in season and out of season; reprove, rebuke, exhort, with great patience and instruction" (2 Timothy 4:2). Likewise, God has given "some as apostles, and some as prophets, and some as evangelists, and some as pastors and teachers, for the equipping of the saints for the work of service" (Ephesians 4:11-12). The question we must address, therefore, is, "What makes a person a *professional* counselor?"

## Training to Be a Counselor

Whether one is a pastor, professional Christian counselor, or lay Christian, there is an absolute standard that can be utilized in training: "All Scripture is inspired by God and profitable for teaching, for reproof, for correction, for training in righteousness; that the man of God may be adequate, equipped for every good work" (2 Timothy 3:16-17). Yet there is more to counseling than simply knowing the Scriptures, and for this reason programs and institutions exist that are designed to train persons to counsel.

In the Christian arena, counseling courses are included in the curricula of Bible colleges, graduate schools, and seminaries. Counseling instruction is usually required to some extent in any ministry-oriented program, including both undergraduate and graduate majors in Bible, theology, and missionary studies. What differs in each major is the number of academic credits required in counseling.

Professional organizations also offer counseling training programs, including the Christian Counseling and Educational Foundation, Emerge Ministries, and the Institute of Pastoral Counseling, as well as broadcast counseling ministries such as "The 700 Club." Finally, many individual churches offer counseling courses that are designed to generally equip "the saints for the work of service" (Ephesians 4:12).

In short, the extent to which counselors are trained range from a short course for the lay person to several years of undergraduate and graduate degree studies.

## Degrees of License

The term *counseling* also covers several professional fields, including psychiatry, psychology, psychotherapy, psychoanalysis, social work, marital and family counseling, and addictions counseling. The many schools of thought identified with counseling often result in an animosity that's based on professional or theological standards. In terms of Christian counseling, the most common grudge appears to be between psychologists and nonpsychologist counselors; indeed the term *Christian psychologist* is often thought to be as much an oxymoron as *Christian lawyer.*

In developing the school of thought known as *Nouthetic* counseling, Jay Adams submits that Scripture should form the *only* standard for counseling practice, to the extent that psychology is an invalid science.[1] In their apologetic for Nouthetic counseling, Martin and Deidre Bobgan refer to the psychological disciplines (including psychological counseling, clinical counseling, psychotherapy, and the psychological aspects of psychiatry) as *psychoheresy*, noting,

> We believe that mental-emotional-behavioral problems of living (nonorganic problems) should be ministered to by biblical encouragement, exhortation, preaching, teaching, and counseling which depends solely upon the truth of God's Word without incorporating the unproven and unscientific psychological opinions of men. Then, if there are biological, medical problems, the person should seek medical rather than psychological assistance.[2]

Counselors such as Adams and the Bobgans essentially write off psychology as secular and of no value, and perhaps end up "throwing the baby out with the bath water." On the other hand, Christian psychologists such as Gary Collins, Larry Crabb, James Dobson, and Clyde and Bruce Narramore recognize that traditional psychology does have value in the counseling arena, *if* and *when* interpreted in light of God's Word.[3]

Although we could argue about the intrinsic legitimacy of psychology in Christian counseling, there is one particular area that is relevant to Christian counselors from a legal perspective: the license to practice. In all fifty states in the nation, psychologists are required to successfully complete

1. See, e.g., Jay E. Adams, *Competent to Counsel* (Phillipsburg, N.J.: Presbyterian & Reformed, 1970).
2. Martin and Deidre Bobgan, *Prophets of Psychoheresy I* (Santa Barbara, Calif.: East Gates, 1989), p. 5.
3. For an excellent treatment of counseling psychology from a Christian perspective, see Gary R. Collins, *Christian Counseling: A Comprehensive Guide* (Waco, Tex: Word, 1980), and Clyde M. Narramore, *The Psychology of Counseling* (Grand Rapids: Zondervan, 1960).

professional board exams and be licensed by the state to practice. Most states require that psychologists graduate from schools approved by the American Psychological Association (similar to the requirement that lawyers graduate from an ABA-approved law school). Additionally, an increasing number of states that formerly allowed persons with a master's degree in psychology to sit for the boards are starting to require a doctoral degree in psychology as a minimum standard.

States that have a licensure law for nonpsychologist counselors include Alabama, Arkansas, Florida, Idaho, North Carolina, Texas, and Virginia.[4] These laws are primarily geared toward secular counselors in agency or private practice, and whether they could include persons engaged in spiritual or religious counseling (as well as persons in a church-based counseling ministry) has not been tested in court. In most other states, however, the only type of counseling professionals required to be licensed are psychiatrists (who, by nature, are licensed as physicians) and psychologists.

From the professional perspective, there are advantages and disadvantages to being a licensed counseling professional. The primary advantage is that, if you have a full-time counseling practice, licensure will provide the means for you to collect third-party insurance payments. The disadvantage is that you will be held to a duty-of-care standard (see chapter 8) and have a higher degree of liability than a nonlicensed counselor. In the *Nally* case, for example, the California Supreme Court ruled that "nontherapist [nonlicensed] counselors" do not have the same duty of care to the client that a licensed psychologist would have.

Occupational titles that are generally not regulated by a licensing requirement include behavioral therapist, counselor, psychotherapist, and psychoanalyst. Thus, we run into a delineation most of the general public is not familiar with: in order to call yourself a psychologist, you must have a graduate-level education and pass the state boards. In most states,

4. Bruce R. Hopkins and Barbara S. Anderson, *The Counselor and the Law* (Alexandria, Va.: AACD Press, 1985), p. 102.

in order to call yourself anything *other* than a psychologist, you need neither a formal education nor a license to practice.

There's good news and bad news in counseling today. The good news is that there are programs available in a multitude of fields designed to make a person competent to counsel. Unfortunately, there are many people practicing who are *incompetent* to counsel.

To take an example in the extreme, I can buy a dog named Fido, call Fido a "psychotherapist," have business cards printed that identify him as such, open a counseling center where people can come and pour out their troubles to Fido, and charge whatever the market will bear.

Even though my own graduate education is in religion and law, I can print business cards that identify me as a psychoanalyst (after all, if someone presumes my doctorate is in a counseling field, who am I to argue?), and engage in a full-time analytical practice with neither state regulation nor my clients being the wiser.

## A Matter of Intent

In the realm of counseling, whether Christian or secular, two types of charlatans are practicing today: those who intend to defraud, and those who sincerely believe they're ordained to do something they're not qualified to do. Legally, then, there is one central point that may determine the liability of a counselor: Is the counselor purporting to be something that he or she is not?

Your best protection as a counselor is not to hold yourself out to be more than you're qualified to be. If you are a trained lay Christian counselor, you should not be purporting to be a professional counselor. If you are a pastor, your business cards should not refer to you as a "professional counselor." The fact that counseling will be a significant part of your pastoral ministry is a given assumption. But your counseling should be in the pastoral context and should not imply credentials that you may not have.

### A Standard for Adjudication

Let's return to our basic question: What makes a person a *professional* counselor? The answer is simple: a professional counselor, *for purposes of liability*, is someone who calls himself or herself a professional counselor. Even in the *Nally* case, the court noted, "Our opinion does not foreclose imposing liability on nontherapist counselors, *who hold themselves out as professionals*, for injuries related to their counseling activities."[5]

In the event of a legal action against you as a counselor, the standard you will be held to in a court of law is that which you hold yourself to in public. Whether you do or do not have the appropriate training for any given field, if you call yourself a professional counselor, you will be held to the standards of the average professional counselor practicing in your community. If you refer to yourself as a psychotherapist, psychoanalyst, crisis counselor, addictions counselor, or any other type of professional, you will be held to the common standard for that field in a court of law.

Educational credentials will also play a significant part in the standard of liability to which a counselor will be held. The person who has had several college courses in counseling will be held to a higher standard than a lay counselor, and someone with a masters or doctorate degree in counseling will be held to a still higher standard.

Pastors and counselors should review their own professional practice and determine whether they are accurately representing their qualifications to parishioners, clients, and the general public. The following questions may be helpful.

1. Does your letterhead, business card, or promotional literature identify you as a professional counselor?
2. Does your literature identify you as having expertise in a particular field (for example, marriage or family counseling)?

5. Nally, 763 P.2d at 961, fn. 8 (italics added).

3. If you are promoting yourself as a professional, how do your educational credentials stack up with similar practitioners in your area? For example, do you have a few undergraduate counseling credits or have you completed a comprehensive program, such as an M.A., in counseling? This is an important delineation. If, for example, you have limited professional education and are called to testify in a court of law, the opposing side may bring in an expert witness who is able to discredit your testimony by means of a more extensive professional education.
4. If you are a pastor, are your counseling services available only to members of your congregation, or do you counsel nonmembers on a regular basis?
5. If you are a pastor, is most of your counseling done on a one-time or occasional basis, or do congregants meet with you for a regularly scheduled weekly appointment?
6. If you meet with individual congregants on a regularly scheduled basis, are the meetings called counseling sessions? (Remember, Kenneth Nally's initial meetings with a pastor at the Grace Community Church were in the context of a "discipling relationship.")[6] If you are referring to the sessions by another name, are they legitimately something other than counseling sessions per se?
7. Do you charge a fee for your counseling services? If so, is it a fixed hourly fee?
8. If your church has a counseling ministry that uses lay counselors, does the church charge a fee to counselees for the services of lay counselors? If so, they may be acting as professional counselors.
9. Even if you are not a professional counselor, are you doing anything by way of omission that might give your clients the impression that you are professional? For example, if a person calls you "Doctor" and you do not have a doctorate degree, are you careful enough to correct him or her?

6. Ibid. at 950.

10. Is your counseling religious in nature to the extent that you regularly use the Bible as a resource? If you're counseling a person with an emotional disturbance and neither referencing Scripture nor coming from a biblical framework, chances are you're engaging in secular, not Christian, counseling.

Remember that in its proper context, a "Christian counselor" is *not* a counselor who happens to be a Christian. Rather, it means a Christian who, on the whole, operates from a biblical framework in his or her counseling practice.

# 5

# Caveat Emptor: Let the Buyer Beware

In lieu of state licensing requirements for professions other than psychology, professional associations exist that provide recognition of professional counseling skills. Secular agencies include the American Association for Marriage and Family Therapy, the American Association of Family Counselors and Mediators, and the National Board for Certified Counselors. Legitimate agencies that certify Christian counselors include the American Association of Pastoral Counselors, the Association of Mental Health Clergy, and the Association of Nouthetic Counselors. Additionally, many states now have certifications, such as the C.A.C. (Certified Addictions Counselor) designation, for those in the alcohol and drug treatment fields.

In the above examples, each organization has established standards for education and supervised counseling experiences designed to ensure that the certified individual is a credible practitioner. However, many training organizations and professional associations have been developed, some of which presume to certify a person as a counseling professional whose certifications hold neither academic nor professional credibility. Many of these are little more than a variant of traditional degree and diploma mills.

Take, for example, the Institute for Christian Living (ICL). Located in New Castle, Pennsylvania, the Institute offers a two-day seminar in several cities around the nation that purports to teach the *Personal Profile System*, a diagnostic instrument that will "help you and your employees understand individual behavior, and that of others, in the work environment or at home."[1] At the conclusion of the workshop, says ICL, "you will be a *Nationally Certified Behavioral Consultant*."[2] The seminar is open to anyone who wishes to attend, whether professionals or laypersons.

What, we might ask, is a "nationally certified behavioral consultant"? Is this a certification recognized by legitimate counseling agencies, accreditation associations, or state licensing boards? Not at all. In fact, the term "nationally certified behavioral consultant" is meaningless. The certification comes from the Institute for Christian Living itself and is unrecognized by any legitimate agency.

I have shown the ICL brochure to counseling professionals, and they have reacted in horror to think that an organization presumes to train a person in the use of a psychological testing instrument in the course of a two-day workshop. Normally, the development and use of such instruments requires a graduate-level education that includes courses in testing and assessment, quantitative and qualitative research, and graduate-level statistics.

The ICL brochure indicates that the organization is endorsed by the United Association of Christian Counselors, the Association of Biblical Counselors, and is affiliated with Logos International. It neglects to mention, however, that the two associations mentioned are not recognized certifying agencies or that Logos International, which also trades as Logos Bible College and Graduate School in California, is an unaccredited correspondence school.

### The Accreditation Hoax

As noted in the last chapter, there are two ways of having an illegitimate counseling ministry. One is to intentionally purport to be something that you're not, and the other is to become a victim of a degree or diploma mill and sincerely

1. Promotional brochure for the Institute for Christian Living, 1989.
2. Ibid. (italics original).

believe you're qualified or certified as a professional counselor.

The risk is especially high in terms of correspondence courses, which, unlike resident courses at a legitimate institution, do not include supervised student counseling experiences. To understand how Christians become the victims of a nonlegitimate training program or diploma mill, it may help to understand how degree mills are formed.

Take, for example, the hypothetical case of the Rev. Dr. Joe Jones. "Doctor" Jones received his mail-order doctorate diploma and ordination from the Universal Life Church, a well-known diploma mill. Viewing himself to be divinely ordained as a counselor, he decides to open a school that will offer correspondence courses designed to train Christian counselors.

The first thing Joe does is to form an entity called *The Jones Institute of Christian Counseling,* which he registers as a nonprofit corporation. Any organization may be incorporated not-for-profit; the incorporators need only certify that except for reasonable salaries, any profits earned by the corporation shall not inure to the benefit of an individual.

Having read a few paperback books in counseling written for laypersons, Joe then proceeds to write a syllabus for each course that he wants to offer, utilizing the books he has read as course textbooks. After the completion of a specified number of courses, Joe will award his "students" an attractive wall diploma naming them "Certified Christian Counseling Specialists."

Finally, he designs a brochure touting his counseling courses as the greatest invention since the wheel and places classified ads in major Christian magazines to announce the opening of his counseling institute. The only thing his school doesn't have yet is a credible sounding endorsement. And that's where accreditation comes into the picture.

Realizing that his school will draw more students (or customers) if it's accredited, Joe Jones then incorporates a *second* organization, which he calls *The International Accrediting Association for Institutes of Christian Counseling.* He may even serve as the president of both the counseling institute and the newly formed accrediting association; no one will know the difference. Then, as president of the accrediting association, Joe accredits his own counseling institute.

Just for good measure, Joe calls the regional accrediting association in his area and asks them to send him forms to apply for accreditation. He then states in his brochure, "We are in dialogue with and are seeking recognition by" the regional association. This is a meaningless statement, since a legitimate accreditor will not recognize an obvious diploma mill. However, Joe has really not lied; he has merely stretched the truth and, therefore, may *legally* make the above statement. The fact that the regional accreditation will not be granted is irrelevant; what's important is the implication of legitimacy to his potential students.

And it works like magic! Joe has a seemingly accredited school to train Christian counselors, is offering correspondence courses touted as the greatest thing since the wheel, and is advertising his product in major Christian magazines. For the realist reading this scenario, however, comes the knowledge that a diploma and certification from Joe's counseling institute plus fifty cents will buy you half a cup of coffee. Without the fifty cents, the diploma and certification are worth nothing.

In his classic book on nontraditional education, Dr. John Bear exposes the sham of nonlegitimate degree and diploma mills. At one point he refers to an organization called the International Accrediting Commission for Schools, Colleges and Theological Seminaries:

> The oddest thing about this apparently sincere organization is that they refuse to reveal which schools they have accredited. While a number of reputable schools claim their accreditation, other cases have come to my attention that give cause for concern. The *Arizona Republic* newspaper, for instance, reported that IACSCTS accredited Eula Wesley University in Phoenix (a school that was run by a security guard from his home, according to that paper) without ever visiting the "campus." And the Executive Director of IACSCTS, Dr. George Reuter, once acknowledged to me that even he was unable to find one of his

accredited schools, the National Graduate School, which operated from a mail forwarding service in St. Louis (presumably a fully-accredited mail forwarding service).[3]

The truth is that there are only two types of accreditation that hold any degree of credibility within the professional or academic worlds. The first is regional accreditation, granted by one of the six academic accrediting associations in the United States approved by both the U.S. Department of Education and the Council on Post-Secondary Accreditation (COPA).[4]

The second type is *professional* accreditation, which applies to particular fields of study and also includes approval by the Department of Education and COPA. In religion, the primary professional accrediting agencies are the American Association of Bible Colleges (AABC) and the Association of Theological Schools in the United States and Canada (ATS). Approved accrediting agencies in the counseling area include the Association for Clinical Pastoral Education (ACPE), the American Psychological Association (APA), and the Council on Social Work Education.

## WHAT ABOUT LEGITIMATE INSTITUTIONS?

If a school or organization is not accredited, that in itself doesn't mean that it's a diploma mill. Some legitimate Bible colleges, for example, believe that to apply for regional accreditation would compromise their doctrinal stand by allowing excessive government entanglement with their programs. Others may choose not to seek accreditation from a regional association but may opt for professional accreditation by the

3. John Bear, *Bear's Guide to Earning Non-Traditional College Degrees*, 10th ed. (Berkeley, Calif.: Ten Speed, 1988), p. 2. This is the most authoritative book available today on nontraditional education. In addition to discussing legitimate alternative degree programs, Bear does an excellent job of exposing diploma and accreditation mills and discussing the importance of legitimate accreditation.
4. These include the Middle States Association of Colleges and Schools, New England Association of Schools and Colleges, North Central Association of Colleges and Schools, Northwest Association of Schools and Colleges, Southern Association of Colleges and Schools, and the Western Association of Schools and Colleges.

American Association of Bible Colleges. At the graduate level, some institutions believe that to hold professional accreditation would compromise their doctrinal stand. The Association of Theological Schools, for example, accredits many liberal seminaries, and some evangelical schools feel that ATS accreditation would be inappropriate to pursue.

In terms of professional training organizations, such as the Christian Counseling and Education Foundation, Emerge Ministries, or the Institute of Pastoral Counseling, the key question to ask is, Do they purport to have an accreditation that is not recognized? In the case of these institutions, which are legitimate, they don't claim accreditation at all; they simply offer quality education in counseling. Rather than presuming to grant a meaningless certification, they simply go about fulfilling their ministry of "equipping the saints for the work of service" (Ephesians 4:12).

Another question to ask is whether the training organization has an affiliation with an accredited institution of higher education. Courses offered by the Christian Counseling and Education Foundation, located in Laverock, Pennsylvania, qualify for graduate-level credit in the counseling programs of Biblical Theological Seminary and Westminster Theological Seminary, both of which are regionally accredited by the Middle States Association. Courses offered by the Institute for Pastoral Counseling, an affiliate of Emerge Ministries in Akron, Ohio, are included in the curriculum of Ashland Theological Seminary, which is regionally accredited by the North Central Association.

Finally, a word should be said about professional associations. While groups such as the American Association of Christian Counselors (AACC) and other membership organizations provide an ongoing affiliation with other Christian counselors, it is important not to use such a membership as a professional credential. AACC membership, for example, is open to "mental health professionals, clergy, and lay leaders who hold a serious interest in counseling."[5] In simple terms, *anyone* can join. Membership in professional associations is

5. American Association of Christian Counselors, membership marketing letter.

not a negative quality, providing the counselor does not purport that the membership acts as a credential or certification.

## HOW TO RECOGNIZE A SHAM

How can one recognize whether a school or organization is legitimate if it doesn't hold an accreditation recognized by the Department of Education and the Council on Post-Secondary Accreditation?[6] The answer is that, when shopping for training resources for yourself, your church staff, or church members, you should ask the following questions:[7]

1. Does the organization purport to certify you in a professional field? If so, is it a legitimate certification?
2. Does the organization's marketing literature make inordinate use of personal testimonies? This is a marketing technique that may work for a Christian diet plan, but it doesn't really tell you anything about the quality of the organization's program or training.
3. Is there more than one member of the same family on the board of directors? This may signify a "home-grown" organization and is often (though not always) an indication of a diploma mill.
4. In listing their own faculty, does the list include where they received their degrees? If not, they may have something to hide.
5. Does the organization attempt to justify *not* being accredited? One school states, "As long as we adhere to the literal-intended [sic] meaning of the Word given to this present dispensation of Grace, it will have God's approval; it will be accredited by Him." That, at best, is using the Lord's name to feign legitimacy.
6. Do an inordinate number of faculty members have more than one doctoral degree, and are those degrees earned or honorary? (The president of one apparent degree mill pur-

6. For a partial list of sham accrediting agencies, see Bear, pp. 40-42.
7. The word *organization* in these questions can be taken to indicate an organization, school, institute, professional association, or any other entity dealing with counseling.

ports to hold the "D.D., D.R.E., Lit.D., Th.D., and Ph.D." Either there's something fishy about his credentials, or he's been in school longer than I've been alive.)

7. Do several of the faculty members have "home-grown" degrees? If an inordinate number hold their own doctoral degrees from that institution, there's something wrong. Legitimate schools generally want to diversify the institutional credentials of their faculty.
8. Does the catalogue or brochure indicate that the organization is "investigating," "has been in dialogue with," "is recognized by," or is "pursuing accreditation with" a legitimate accrediting body? Such a statement gives no indication about its chance for achieving accreditation and ultimately means nothing. John Bear reflects, "I can state just as accurately that I am practicing my tennis game, with the intention of playing Ivan Lendl in the finals at Wimbledon. Don't hold your breath."[8]
9. Does the organization say only that it is a nonprofit corporation or that it has "full I.R.S. privileges"? These, too, mean nothing. All churches are federally tax exempt by their very nature, and nonprofit incorporation for organizations other than churches does not, in itself, include tax exemption. The question is whether they have specifically been granted a recognition letter by the I.R.S. confirming their exempt status under Section 501(c)(3) of the Internal Revenue Code. If they have been granted the 501(c)(3) exemption, they don't have to disguise the language.
10. Does the organization place an undue emphasis on an "attractive wall certificate," membership card, or other outward expression of their credentials? If so, they're probably spending more money on the certificate than on the quality of their program. (This is especially true of "ministerial associations" and "mail order churches" that purport to offer "ordination credentials for independent ministers.")

8. Bear, p. 42.

## The Bottom Line: Legitimacy

You must be the final arbiter of whether you are competent to counsel. If, in fact, God has called you to engage in a counseling ministry, whether full-time or part-time, lay or professional, the most important thing is to recognize both your gifts *and* your limitations and not purport to be more than you are.

In addition to the ethical problems presented and the potential pitfalls for the persons being counseled, in today's age of litigation you could feel the negative ramifications of overstating your credentials in a court of law. Legitimacy must be of utmost importance for the Christian counselor, "that you may prove yourselves to be blameless and innocent, children of God above reproach in the midst of a crooked and perverse generation, among whom you appear as lights in the world" (Philippians 2:15).

# 6

# Anatomy of a Church Lawsuit

Contrary to common belief today, lawsuits against churches are not a new trend. People have always sued churches. What's new is *how* they sue churches.

## Lawsuits Then

Imagine the case of John Doe. In the 1940s, John sued the First Baptist Church after the board of elders gave him the "left foot of fellowship." John, it seems, was having an affair with a woman from outside the church.

After his dismissal was announced to the congregation John sued the First Baptist Church, seeking to have his membership reinstated. "After all," John reasoned, "my parents were members of First Baptist. And my grandparents, and my great-grandparents. I have just as much a right to carry on that family tradition."

Taking the church to court, John was able to demonstrate that when the church dismissed him, they did not follow the proper procedure for removing a person from membership. That procedure, outlined in the church's constitution and bylaws, mandated a multi-step process for church discipline that wasn't followed in the heat of the controversy between John and the elders.

The issue of John's dismissal—his sexual affair—was not an issue in the suit. It wasn't necessary to mention it from a legal standpoint; John won his case based on neutral principles of law—the failure of the church to follow its own documented procedures in disciplining a member. The judge ruled that John Doe deserved to be reinstated to membership in the church.

On the Sunday morning following the trial, John took his seat in the church's sanctuary. Nothing had changed; in fact, John's sexual affair had continued throughout the trial.

And so, the First Baptist Church began disciplinary action against him again. This time, however, the elders were careful to follow the multi-step process outlined in their organizational documents. And, in the end, John Doe was once more given the left foot of fellowship. John Doe had won the battle but lost the war.

## Lawsuits Now

It's fifty years later, and John Doe, Jr., is a member of the First Baptist Church. Half a century after his father was disfellowshipped from the same church, the elders of First Baptist find out that John, Jr., is having an affair with a woman from outside the church.

And so the disciplinary process begins. Remembering the lawsuit that shook the church fifty years earlier, the church is much more careful in carrying out its disciplinary policies these days. Following the dictates of Matthew 18, carefully outlined in the church's constitution, the elders meet with him both individually and corporately to seek his repentance and restoration into the congregation. When John, Jr., informs them that the affair is none of their business and that he plans on its continuance, the elders announce to the congregation his dismissal from membership.

And, like his father before him, John Doe, Jr., sues the First Baptist Church. But unlike his father, who sued to be reinstated on the church membership roll, John, Jr., claims that the elders have caused him severe emotional distress by invading his privacy, and he is seeking monetary damages in the amount of five million dollars.

## Changes in Church and Society

When the American Bar Association called litigation against churches an "explosive new area of law," they were half right. People had always sued churches, but the *way* in which they were now suing *was* both explosive and new. For the first time, people began suing churches under the principles of *tort law,*[1] seeking monetary damages for the wrongs they perceived against them. The method was new, and the number of lawsuits against churches has exploded during the last decade.

The advent of tort suits against churches can be attributed to several factors. The first is a general erosion of respect for religious institutions in American society. Writer Tom Wolfe coined the phrase *The "Me" Decade* in the 1970s, and this mind-set continues into the 1990s. People are "looking out for number one," which in this case is themselves, not Jesus Christ. Theologically, it would not be inappropriate to say that many people in the Christian church have removed Jesus from the throne of their lives, replacing Him with themselves. We live in a society where all too often, when requested to commit ourselves to Jesus or to some type of Christian service, we ask, "What's in it for *me*?"

Complicating the public perception of religious institutions has been the prominent scandals that have hit major ministries over the past decade. The Bakker and Swaggart affairs reflected poorly on both parachurch ministries and the Christian church as a whole. At the other end of the spectrum, Jerry Falwell sued publisher Larry Flynt and *Hustler* magazine for emotional distress based on an advertising parody implying that Falwell had sex with his mother in an out-

1. A *tort* is defined as a wrong committed by one person against another. Tort cases are civil rather than criminal in nature and cover any area in which a person is wronged, with the exception of breach of contract. Torts generally consist of a legal obligation, a breach of that obligation, and damage as a result of that breach.

house.[2] While Falwell's reaction, and the suit, may have been justified, an underlying message was communicated: if a pastor could sue a person for emotional distress, why couldn't it occur the other way around?

Second, there has been a significant overall increase in tort claims in the United States over the past decade, especially in the area of personal injury litigation. A contributing element in this increase has been the implementation of media advertising by attorneys, who tell us that if we are in an accident we can collect damages for pain and suffering, lost wages, inconvenience, etc. We have become one of the most litigious societies in the world, one in which it's almost considered a sin *not* to sue.

Television has contributed significantly to this mind-set. "L.A. Law" and other programs regularly demonstrate that the judicial system provides the ultimate satisfaction for avenging ourselves. "The People's Court" exhorts us when we are wronged, "Don't take matters into your own hands; take them to court." In addition to the secular media, advertising by personal injury attorneys now appears on Christian radio stations around the nation.

The third factor is an erosion of a legal doctrine known as *charitable immunity.* Under the charitable immunity doctrine, if I donated money to a church in the form of a tithe or offering, I had the assurance that my money would be used for the purpose I intended when I made the contribution: the support of the church and the furtherance of the gospel.[3] Over

2. Hustler Magazine and Larry C. Flynt v. Jerry Falwell, 485 U.S. 46 (1988). Falwell won the suit at the district court level and was awarded substantial damages for invasion of privacy and intentional infliction of emotional distress. The judgment was affirmed by the U.S. Court of Appeals, but the U.S. Supreme Court reversed the lower courts on the grounds that, since Falwell is a public figure, *Hustler* magazine was protected by the First Amendment regardless of how distasteful the ad parody was. For a comprehensive history of the case, see Rodney A. Smolla, *Jerry Falwell v. Larry Flynt: The First Amendment on Trial* (New York: St. Martins, 1988).
3. The same principle applied to any charitable organization that was tax exempt under Section 501(c)(3) of the Internal Revenue Code. This included educational institutions, hospitals, missionary organizations, and human service organizations. Therefore, changes in this area of law have had a significant impact on both churches and nonreligious institutions.

the past decade, the courts in the United States have eroded the charitable immunity doctrine to the extent that there is no longer an assurance that moneys donated for a specified purpose (e.g., the spread of the gospel) will not be used to pay damages in a lawsuit.

Finally, the advent of clergy malpractice insurance has proved a mixed blessing for churches and individual pastors. Although the tort of clergy malpractice per se was rejected in the *Nally* case, churches and individuals can still be held liable for negligence or other kinds of malpractice. The good news is that clergy malpractice insurance will usually cover the costs of defending a church or pastor in a lawsuit. The bad news is that the existence of malpractice coverage in a church's insurance policy creates a "deep pocket" that invites litigation against the church.[4]

## Going for the Deep Pocket

When a person files a tort claim to seek damages for a perceived injury, liability is spread as far as possible to ensure an award. Though the law in the United States presumes innocence until guilt is proved, a number of factors indicate that a person filing a lawsuit will often be awarded damages whether or not the party being sued is actually guilty of malpractice or negligence. The bottom line: even though a church may be found innocent in a lawsuit, the toll against the church can still be an expensive one.

Imagine the case of Jane Smith. On the way into church one Sunday morning, the heel of Jane's shoe breaks and she falls on the sidewalk, fracturing her ankle. It's snowing as she falls, and the snow may or may not have contributed to the accident. Meanwhile, Jane is forced to stay at home for several weeks, missing work while her ankle heals. Not having anything better to do, Jane is watching television one day and

4. The advent of malpractice insurance, which invites lawsuits, is by no means limited to pastoral counselors. In 1990, the American Psychological Association's Insurance Trust announced a 50 percent increase in malpractice premiums, largely as a result of sexual misconduct claims against psychologists. (See Youngstrom, p. 16.)

sees a commercial featuring Bob Johnson, a local attorney, who tells her that she may be able to collect damages for her injury. Not only can she collect, but Bob's services will not cost anything until she wins her case.[5] Jane thinks this is an attractive deal, and Bob begins proceedings to seek damages for Jane's injury.

The first thing Bob Johnson does is identify all parties that might be held liable for negligence that would have contributed to Jane's broken ankle. That the church could be held liable is obvious, since Jane fell on the church's property. But there are other parties that might also be held liable, such as the manufacturer of Jane's shoes. After all, a manufacturing defect might have contributed to the broken heel. Bob will also name the store at which Jane bought the shoes as a codefendant, since they may have been selling defective merchandise.

If the church is incorporated, the church staff members may be protected from individual liability. But if the church is an unincorporated association, the individuals may be held liable. Therefore, Bob includes the pastor in the damage claim. If the church employs a janitor or groundskeeper, that person will also be included on the assumption that he didn't fulfill his job responsibilities by shoveling the sidewalk leading to the church.

We now have five defendants: the church as an association, the church's pastor and janitor individually, the shoe manufacturer, and the shoe store. Even if one or two of them are judged to be innocent of negligence, there are still a few left who can be held liable.

After estimating the losses Jane has suffered, as well as how much time he will invest in seeking an award as a result of her fall, Bob recommends suing for $100,000 in damages. Determining that all five of the parties are insured, Bob then

5. This is known in law as a contingency fee. An attorney who accepts a personal injury case on a contingency basis earns his or her fee if the litigation is successful, whether in or out of court. Standard contingency fees are in the 30-40 percent range if a lawsuit is settled out of court, or 40-50 percent if the case goes to trial. However, even in contingency fee-based cases, the client is normally required to pay up front for court costs (e.g., filing fees) and out-of-pocket expenses such as fees charged by a private investigator.

contacts their insurance companies to negotiate a settlement for Jane.

### Insurance: A Guaranteed Victory for the Plaintiff

Insurance companies are masters of actuarial science; they can put the best of Las Vegas gamblers to shame with their skills in computing the odds that determine how profitable the insurance industry will be. As Bob Johnson has computed the time and money involved in seeking an award for Jane Smith, the insurance companies that represent the church and its staff, the shoe manufacturer, and the shoe store begin to compute the cost of defending their insured parties in Jane's lawsuit.

Jane's church is insured by the ABC Insurance Company, and the policy covers the acts of the pastor and church janitor as individuals. All things being equal, let's assume that the potential liability for these three out of five defendants is $60,000. The staff attorney at ABC Insurance speculates that since it was actually snowing at the time of Jane's fall, it is prudent to assume that the church did not have the responsibility of shoveling the sidewalk until the snow stopped. Therefore, the insurance company feels that if the case goes to trial, the church and its staff will be found innocent of negligence.

However, taking the case to trial requires an enormous expenditure of money to research the facts of the case, write and file briefs, engage in discovery proceedings (including the gathering of evidence and the taking of depositions from the opposing parties). The insurance company may hire an investigator to verify that Jane Smith actually has suffered an injury, paying the investigator an hourly fee to sit in a car outside of Jane's house with a video camera, hoping to catch her playing tennis with her broken ankle and proving that she is not as injured as she claims to be.

In the meantime, the charges will be amended, additional briefs will be filed, and the jury selection process and preparation of arguments will take up the insurance attorney's time before the case is even heard. In short, the pre-trial expenses will amount to a substantial expenditure even if the church and its staff are found innocent of liability.

Additionally, the insurer knows that people on juries are often persuaded by personalities, not issues or evidence, and that juries are often sympathetic to the plaintiff even if negligence doesn't exist. After considering the case of Jane Smith, the ABC Insurance Company projects their defense costs to be in the range of $25,000. Therefore, even if the insured parties are found innocent, the insurer is guaranteed to take a loss.

### A Little Something for Your Trouble

Jim Scott, claims investigator for the ABC Insurance Company, has determined that Jane Smith has suffered a legitimate loss in terms of medical expenses, lost wages, and the price of the shoes on which a heel broke. He estimates that ABC's potential liability for her actual injury amounts to $5,000 (not including additional damages for pain and suffering).

A common calculation in the insurance industry is to multiply the actual loss threefold: one-third to cover each of the plaintiff's loss, pain and suffering, and the contingency fee for the plaintiff's attorney. Therefore, Jim offers Bob Johnson, Jane's attorney, an out-of-court settlement of $15,000. The offer is accepted, and the case is settled.

The $5,000 covering Jane's medical bills, lost wages, and damaged shoes has been paid, and she has received another $5,000 for her pain and suffering. Bob Johnson, who based his contingency fee on one-third of the total award, has earned $5,000 for his work on behalf of Jane, and has not even had to argue the case in court. The insurance company, which would have had to pay $25,000 in expenses even if they weren't found liable, has saved $10,000 (not to mention an additional $60,000 in damages if they had been found liable in court).

Everyone is happy. Even the church is happy—at least for the moment. Chances are that their insurance premiums will skyrocket when the policy is renewed. *If* the policy is renewed.

The scenario presented here makes it relatively easy to gauge damages. Jane Smith suffered a specific injury, which resulted in specific medical expenses and loss of wages. In the case of a lawsuit based on counseling malpractice or negligence, however, the injury can be more difficult to gauge, and the damages can be more severe. But it's reasonable to conclude that any time a lawsuit is filed, there's a good chance that the plaintiff will receive an award, even if negligence has not occurred or the suit does not go to court.

# 7

# Confidentiality and Privileged Communications

There are many elements in a successful counseling relationship. These include the willingness of the counselee to seek help, the competence of the counselor, and the confidentiality of the counseling relationship. It is important to note here that most of the principles outlined in this chapter refer specifically to the confidentiality privilege between minister and penitent. Most, though not all, states do not recognize a confidentiality privilege for lay or professional Christian counselors who are not pastors. Likewise, for pastoral counselors it is important to keep in mind that the confidentiality privilege may apply only to specific counseling situations, e.g., when the minister is specifically acting in a pastoral role.

In terms of pastoral counseling, confidentiality has its historical base in the Roman Catholic sacrament of confession:

> The sacramental seal is inviolable. Accordingly, it is absolutely wrong for a confessor in any way to betray the penitent, for any reason whatsoever, whether by word or in any other fashion. The confessor is wholly forbidden to use knowledge acquired in confession to the detriment of the penitent, even when all danger of disclosure is excluded.[1]

1. Code of Canon Law, Canons 983-84.

Confession itself is not limited to a sacrament in the Roman Catholic church and is, in fact, biblical in origin. As the people of Jerusalem and elsewhere went out to John the Baptist in the Judean wilderness, we read that "they were being baptized by him in the Jordan River, as they confessed their sins" (Matthew 3:6; Mark 1:5). Both Jews and Greeks in Ephesus became believers and openly confessed their former practices (Acts 19:18).

Christians are exhorted by James to "confess your sins to one another, and pray for one another, so that you may be healed" (James 5:16). In the ministry of the church, confession is also an expression of the ministry of reconciliation (2 Corinthians 5:18-19). Jesus spoke of the law of reconciliation: "If therefore you are presenting your offering at the altar, and there remember that your brother has something against you, leave your offering there before the altar, and go your way, first be reconciled to your brother, and then come and present your offering" (Matthew 5:23-24).

Yet another expression of confession can be found in the counseling relationship. The goal of Christian counseling, ultimately, is to restore and reconcile a believer to fellowship and healthy relationships in a biblical context. From a legal perspective, the confidentiality privilege cannot be limited to the Roman Catholic church, nor can a civil court determine whether confession can be treated as a sacrament, ordinance, or biblically mandated procedure in any denomination. In short, what is legally acceptable for any one church must be acceptable for any other church. This is based on the principle that civil courts cannot favor any one church over another, for "the law knows no heresy, and is committed to the support of no dogma, the establishment of no sect."[2]

### CONFIDENTIALITY VERSUS PRIVILEGED COMMUNICATION

Confidentiality is best defined as an ethical decision not to reveal what is learned in the context of a professional relationship, e.g., that between the counselor and the counselee.

2. Watson v. Jones, 80 U.S. (13 Wall.) 679, 728 (1872).

Confidentiality is traditional in nature, and, while it enjoys historical protection, it has no legal protection.

A privileged communication, on the other hand, is the same as confidentiality, but it is codified in law. Under a privileged communication statute, a minister acting in his professional capacity as a spiritual advisor cannot be forced to reveal the content of confidential communications to any outside party, including a court of law. A typical confidentiality statute for clergy reads as follows:

> No clergyman, priest, rabbi or minister of the gospel of any regularly established church or religious organization, except clergymen or ministers who are self-ordained or who are members of religious organizations in which members other than the leader thereof are deemed clergymen or ministers, who while in the course of his duties has acquired information from any person secretly and in confidence shall be compelled, or allowed without consent of such person, to disclose that information in any legal proceeding, trial or investigation before any government unit.[3]

This confidentiality privilege for clergy includes two items of note. First, the privilege is not limited to the Roman Catholic sacrament of confession; it includes any clergyman in any established church. Second, the privilege does *not* include clergy who are self-ordained (such as members of the Universal Life Church, which ordains individuals by mail for a fee) or members of religious organizations such as the Jehovah's Witnesses, in which all members are considered clergy.

Confidentiality privileges in most states are not limited to clergy. Other occupations often covered by statute include attorneys, journalists (insofar as they are not required to disclose their sources of information), physicians, licensed psychologists, school personnel (including guidance counselors, school nurses, home and school visitors, and related clerical staff), addictions counselors, and sexual assault counselors.

Privileged communication statutes are generally established at the state level, and most courts perceive that the

3. 42 Pa.C.S.A. 5943 (1978).

establishment of the privilege is a legislative responsibility. Thus, courts will generally not recognize a confidentiality privilege unless it is codified by the local state legislature.

Rule 505 of the Federal Rules of Evidence also establishes a federal confidentiality privilege for clergy:

> (a) Definitions. As used in this rule:
>
> (1) A "clergyman" is a minister, priest, rabbi, accredited Christian Science Practitioner, or other similar functionary of a religious organization, or an individual reasonably believed to so be by the person consulting him.
>
> (2) A communication is "confidential" if made privately and not intended for further disclosure except to other persons present in furtherance of the purpose of the communication.
>
> (b) General rule of privilege. A person has a privilege to refuse to disclose and to prevent another from disclosing a confidential communication by the person to a clergyman in his professional character as spiritual advisor.
>
> (c) Who may claim the privilege. The privilege may be claimed by the person, by his guardian or conservator, or by his personal representative if he is deceased. The person who was the clergyman at the time of the communication is presumed to have authority to claim the privilege but only on behalf of the communicant.[4]

The federal privilege, however, is often not applied in light of a separate rule that, when an element of a claim or defense is determined by state law, the federal court should defer to the applicable laws of the individual state.[5]

## Scope of the Confidentiality Privilege

By definition, the confidentiality privilege protects the person making a confession or being counseled; protection for the pastor is secondary. The privilege provides an assurance that facts disclosed to a pastor will not be revealed by that pastor in the context of court testimony.

4. Uniform Rules of Evidence, Rule 505 (1974).
5. Ibid., Rule 501.

Confidentiality as an ethical principle goes farther than a privileged communication statute; it ensures that the facts disclosed will not be relayed to anyone outside of the confessional or counseling relationship. The scope of privileged communication statutes for clergy differs from state to state, and may range from a penitential communication made in a confessional relationship to the wider counseling relationship in general.

In Colorado, for example, "a clergyman or priest shall not be examined without the consent of the person making the confession as to any confession made to him in his professional character in the course of discipline enjoined by the church to which he belongs."[6] Maryland, on the other hand, recognizes a broader privilege that includes any spiritual counseling: "A minister of the gospel, clergyman, or priest of an established church of any denomination may not be compelled to testify on any matter in relation to any confession or communication made to him in confidence by a person seeking his spiritual advice or consolation."[7] Likewise, states may restrict the confidentiality privilege to testimony in civil trials or criminal trials, or may allow the privilege to be claimed in both types of proceedings.

The distinction between the *confessional* relationship and the *counseling* relationship is important here, since counseling is broader than confession and may include statements of the confider's past conduct, confessions, expressions of repentance, expressions of anger and other deeply felt emotions, solicitations of advice, personal background information, and statements about the wrongdoings of others.[8]

The pastoral role also helps define the scope of the privilege. Thus, communications made to nonpastors do not enjoy the confidentiality privilege in most states. Nonpastors include elders, deacons, unordained youth ministers, nuns, unordained professional counselors, and lay counselors.

6. Colo. Rev. Stat. 13-90-107(c) (1973).
7. Md. Cts. & Jud. Proc. Code Ann. 9-111 (1984).
8. Mary Harter Mitchell, "Must Clergy Tell? Child Abuse Reporting Requirements Versus the Clergy Privilege and Free Exercise of Religion," *Minnesota Law Review* 71 (1987): 748.

The applicability of the privilege may also be made on the basis of whether the clergyman is ordained, licensed, or commissioned, or whether serving in a pastoral or nonpastoral capacity (e.g., in a parachurch ministry). For example, the pastor of an independent church, even though not ordained, may be protected based on his pastoral role. Also, nonclergy persons on the counseling staff of a church may be protected if acting on behalf of the pastor (e.g., if the counseling load is too large for the pastor).

Finally, in order for a communication to be covered by the privilege, the minister must have heard it in his professional role as a pastor or spiritual advisor. The key to understanding this context is in the term minister-*penitent* relationship. A legal dilemma is faced when the minister is not acting in a pastoral capacity or when the counseling is not penitential. In Alabama, for example, a man confessed the murder of his girlfriend to a local pastor. The minister reported the man to the police, and the man's lawyer attempted to have the evidence barred from trial based on the clergy-penitent privilege. The court held that the evidence was admissible, ruling that when the man made the confession at the minister's home he was seeking refuge from the police and was not making a penitential confession.[9]

Therefore, time and place play a significant role in whether a communication is covered by the confidentiality privilege, with maximum protection afforded to formal confessional or counseling sessions. According to attorney Richard Hammar:

> Many, perhaps most, of the communications made to a minister are not made to him in his professional capacity as a spiritual adviser. They are made to him, by church members and nonmembers alike, at church functions, following church services, in committee rooms, in hospital rooms, at funeral homes, on street corners, and at social and recreational events. Such communications ordinarily are not privileged. Even strictly

9. Lucy v. State, 443 So.2d 1335 (Crim. App. Ala. 1983).

private conversations may be made for purposes other than spiritual advice, and these are not privileged.[10]

## Exceptions to the Confidentiality Privilege

Several legal exceptions apply to the confidentiality privilege in general, though in some of them the parties to whom confidential communications are disclosed are also bound by the privilege.

The most significant exception is when a disclosure indicates that a counselee may pose a danger to self or others (see chapter 8). Courts have established a duty to warn third parties of possible danger (e.g., by a homicidal counselee) and to seek involuntary commitment by a potentially suicidal counselee. In such instances, the confidentiality privilege for professional counselors is abrogated.

Likewise, many states require the reporting of cases of child abuse, whether confirmed or reasonably suspected. States differ on whether the reporting requirements include clergy counselors who learn of an abuse situation in the course of penitential counseling (see chapter 11).

The confidentiality privilege may also be abrogated when disclosure is requested by the counselee. Absent a claim of privilege, in most states even clergy counselors must disclose the information at the counselee's request. Attorney Mary Harter Mitchell illustrates how different versions of a privileged communication statute would dictate disclosure in different situations (see chart on page 78). When, in a certain situation, the counselee has requested disclosure of confidential information, it is advisable to obtain a written authorization (or "Consent to Disclosure") from the counselee for the release of the information, to be kept on file by the counselor.

Clinical supervision is another exception to the confidentiality privilege. Professional counseling or psychology programs generally require a supervised practicum or internship. This would include, for example, masters-level counseling programs at Christian seminaries. In a practicum con-

10. Richard R. Hammar, *Pastor, Church & Law* (Springfield, Mo.: Gospel Publishing, 1983), pp. 54-55.

| VERSION OF PRIVILEGE | Cleric Willing to Tell; Confider Willing, Too | Cleric Willing to Tell; Confider Objects | Cleric Objects to Telling; Confider Willing | Cleric Objects to Telling; Confider Objects, Too |
|---|---|---|---|---|
| Clergy may not disclose | no disclosure | no disclosure | no disclosure | no disclosure |
| Clergy may not disclose without confider's consent | disclosure | no disclosure | disclosure | no disclosure |
| Clergy may not be compelled to disclose | disclosure | disclosure | no disclosure | no disclosure |
| Clergy may not be compelled to disclose without confider's consent[11] | disclosure | disclosure | disclosure | no disclosure |

text, the counseling intern usually shares details of his or her work with a supervisor. In this situation, however, the supervisor is also bound by the confidentiality privilege. Likewise, counseling notes may be typed or otherwise accessed by secretaries or clerical assistants. In this situation, such a person becomes a "clerical extension" of the counselor and is also bound by the confidentiality privilege.

Professional consultations provide another exception to the rule. Even pastoral counselors require professional consultations in order to deal with difficult counseling situations, whether that help is sought from a professional counselor or another minister, and such consultations are often in the best interest of the counselee. Again, the professional consulted would be bound by the privilege.

Finally, communications made with a third party present are not considered to be protected by the confidentiality privilege. This includes group counseling sessions, training

11. Mitchell, p. 756.

sessions for other counselors who share details of their own lives, or sessions in which any other person is present.[12]

### Confidentiality and Non-Clergy Counselors

Whether Christian counselors who are not acting in a pastoral capacity are protected by the confidentiality privilege is determined by (1) whether an individual state protects the counselor-client relationship by statute, and/or (2) whether the state has licensing laws for professional counselors. One secular counseling text reports that fifteen states offer privileged protection to at least some nonpsychologist counselors: Connecticut, Delaware, Idaho, Indiana, Kentucky, Maine, Michigan, Montana, Nevada, North Carolina, North Dakota, Oklahoma, Oregon, Pennsylvania, and South Dakota. The authors also note that Virginia is an example of a state that has granted privileged communication rights to licensed professional counselors, social workers, and psychologists in civil cases, not criminal proceedings.[13]

It is important, however, that counselors carefully check the laws in their individual states. Pennsylvania, for example, protects school counselors and sexual abuse counselors, but not professional Christian counselors. Therefore, even the laws of states that protect some nonpsychologist counselors may not include religious counselors unless they are covered by ministerial status or the pastoral role.

Likewise, it is important to differentiate between licensed secular counselors and Christian counselors. Since Christian counselors generally base their approach on Scripture, it is improbable that a licensing requirement for biblically based counselors would be found constitutional.

For the professional or lay Christian counselor, then, there's good news and bad news. The good news is that a licensing requirement is unlikely to be imposed by any state.

12. A possible exception to this would be a session between a male pastor and female counselee in which the office door is kept open and a church secretary in the outer office may overhear the session. This has not been tested at trial, but it is likely that a court would recognize this as a privileged communication.
13. Dean L. Hummel, Lou C. Talbott, and M. David Alexander, *Law and Ethics in Counseling* (New York: Van Nostrand Reinhold, 1985), p. 56.

The bad news is that nonclergy Christian counselors are not likely to be protected by most states' privileged communication statutes. However, in those states that have a licensing requirement for professional counselors, the Christian counselor who meets the licensing standard might wish to consider becoming licensed in order to be protected by a statute applicable to counselors in general.

Even if not covered by a confidentiality privilege, a court may be lenient in the event that a Christian counselor refuses to disclose information based on sincerely held religious belief. This possibility will depend largely on the nature of the issue at trial. For example, nondisclosure of a child abuse situation by a Christian counselor is likely to be dealt with more harshly than not disclosing information about a marriage relationship in a divorce proceeding.

There may also be a situation in which biblical admonitions for reconciliation and dealing with a problem within a church (or, perhaps, the mandate against litigation between Christians in 1 Corinthians 6:1-7) may preclude a counselor from testifying at trial, even if he or she is not protected by the confidentiality privilege. In this event, there may also be a civil or criminal penalty for refusal to testify. That, however, is a matter for prayer, discernment, and consultation with an attorney.

At the other end of the spectrum is the need to disclose information at the congregational level in the case of church discipline. In this situation, the disclosure of information by either a clergy or nonclergy counselor could result in litigation by the counselee against the church, counseling agency, and/or individual counselor (see chapter 10).

## A POSSIBLE SOLUTION: INFORMED CONSENT

The legal ramifications of disclosing confidential material include lawsuits based on invasion of privacy, outrageous conduct on the part of the counselor, and infliction of emotional distress. One possible solution to this dilemma is to obtain an acknowledgment of informed consent from the counselee, preferably in writing, at the beginning of the counseling relationship.

Informed consent would cover the commitment on the part of the counselor to disclose any information to appropriate authorities or persons in the church in the event of a danger to self or others (e.g., potential suicide or homicide) or—in the case of church discipline—unrepented sin. If, for example, a person having an adulterous affair is seeking counseling, it is likely that he or she is approaching the counseling in a penitential framework. However, if the affair continues after significant counseling has taken place, the guidelines of Matthew 18:15-17 require that the situation be dealt with in the context of church discipline. The presence of informed consent in the counseling relationship could serve to protect the counselor (and his or her church or agency) in the discipline process.

The bad news about written informed consent is that it can contribute to a chilling effect in the counseling relationship, in which the counselee is not as open as he or she might be if assured that information revealed to the counselor will not be disclosed under any circumstance. Logistically, a chilling effect is also created if a pastor presents a parishioner with an informed consent form prior to initiating a formal counseling relationship, even if that parishioner had disclosed personal information to the pastor previously. One solution to alleviating the chilling effect is to include a blanket statement in a church's constitution or bylaws to the effect that the Matthew 18 standards are utilized as a guideline for church discipline and that discipline may include actions based on information that is revealed in a confidential setting.

For a parachurch agency engaged in counseling, an alternative to written informed consent is to discuss the agency's disclosure policy at the beginning of the counseling relationship. In this circumstance, it is advisable for the counselor to sign a form indicating that the scope of confidentiality was discussed with the counselee prior to beginning formal counseling. This would ensure that the discussion of the policy is documented in the agency's file and that the policy is discussed on a consistent basis.

# 8

# Counseling Malpractice and Negligence

The *Nally* case held that Christian counselors do not have a duty of care to a person in a pastoral counseling situation. However, since *Nally* was decided by the California Supreme Court, its impact is binding only in the state of California.

The American judicial system works on the principle of *stare decisis*, the "principle of precedent." Under *stare decisis*, when a court decides a case, the ruling in that case acts as a precedent for similar cases that come before the court later. The *Nally* case is a precedent to the degree that it was the first significant case heard in the United States charging clergy malpractice per se. Future cases that are similar will, if heard in California, be decided by relying on *Nally* as a ruling precedent.

However, no other state is bound by the *Nally* decision. If a similar case arises in another state, the court *may* look to *Nally* for guidance, but it is not obliged to do so. Therefore, it is possible that in counseling malpractice cases brought in other states, the courts will find that a duty of care does exist. If the church or counselor being sued is perceived by the court not to have met that duty, the church will be held liable.

As churches are sued successfully on issues such as church discipline, defamation, and seduction, it is perhaps only a matter of time before they are held liable for malpractice in the counseling area. Therefore, this chapter assumes that despite the *Nally* ruling in favor of the Grace Community Church, churches are not likely to be found as innocent in the future. Because courts are unpredictable in their rulings and juries tend to rule in favor of the plaintiff when they perceive an injury has occurred (whether or not the plaintiff is at fault), it is important to understand the elements of a successful malpractice lawsuit in the counseling arena.

For purposes of this chapter, the terms *malpractice* and *negligence* are used interchangeably. Likewise, the terms *client* and *counselee* can be used interchangeably. Normally, a *client* is someone who is being counseled by a professional psychologist or counselor, whereas *counselee* can also refer to a pastoral or Christian counseling relationship.

## Elements of a Negligence Suit

For a counselor to be successfully sued, four conditions must be present: duty of care, breach of duty, injury, and proximate cause.

*Duty of care* can be defined as a special relationship between you as the counseling professional (the "counselor") and the person being counseled (the "client"), to the extent that you are considered to have a responsibility to ensure the client's safety and welfare. Courts have found this to include the responsibility to prevent the client from harming him or herself, as well as preventing the client from harming another person.

*Breach of duty* can occur in two ways: you, as the counselor, do something that you shouldn't do, or you don't do something you should do to ensure the welfare of the client or another person threatened by injury. The standard for defining a breach of duty is what the average prudent person in your professional capacity would do in a similar situation.

Doing something you shouldn't do generally takes the form of sexual involvement and often occurs in a marriage counseling situation. An individual or couple comes to you for counseling, and you have an affair with a counselee. While we don't like to admit that this happens in the realm of Christian counseling, the sad fact is that many successful lawsuits against counselors, including the clergy, have been based on seduction. This breach of duty is generally considered intentional in nature.

Not doing something you should do is usually unintentional and includes referring clients to other competent counselors in the event that you are unable to counsel them successfully, seeking the commitment of a client who is suicidal, or warning a third party of possible danger if the client is homicidal. Note, however, that the responsibility of effecting the institutional commitment of a person generally applies only to licensed counseling professionals who have the professional affiliation and means to facilitate the process; the duty to commit has not been applied to pastoral or other Christian counselors.

An *injury* can be defined as harm done to a person's physical or mental well-being, harm to one's pride or reputation, or harm to one's rights and privileges. For a suit to be successful, it must be proved that your breach of the duty of care was the *proximate cause* (direct cause) of the injury. A severely disturbed parishioner or client often poses a danger to person or property. The catch-phrase normally used in counseling is "danger to self or others," though others can also include property or other nonpersons.

## Danger to Self

A person is considered a danger to self if he or she is found to be potentially suicidal. In reviewing the case of Ken Nally, the California Supreme Court observed that that Dr. John Hall, a physician and deacon at Grace Community Church, recognized Ken's suicidal tendencies. He offered to arrange for Ken's involuntary commitment, but the offer was rejected by Ken's mother, who opposed psychiatric hospitalization for her son, saying, "No, that's a crazy hospital. He's not crazy."[1]

In most states, licensed physicians and psychologists have a duty to take precautions to prevent suicide in the lim-

1. Nally, 763 P.2d at 951-52.

ited context of hospital-patient relationships wherein the suicidal person is under the care and custody of physicians and staff who are aware of an unstable mental condition. Additionally, if a physician or psychologist becomes aware of suicidal tendencies in an outpatient relationship, he or she has a duty to seek the involuntary commitment of that person to prevent the patient from carrying out a suicide threat.

### Danger to Specified Others

A danger to other persons can be broken down into two categories: danger to a *specified other*, and danger to an *unspecfied other.*

Danger to a *specified other* occurs when a counselee makes a threat to do bodily harm to a specific, identifiable person or persons, e.g., "I'm going to kill my (wife/husband/parent/child)." Courts have ruled that when such a threat is made and the counseling professional believes there is an indication that it may be acted upon, the counselor is obligated not only to report the possibility of such an action to the police but also to warn the intended victim. This requires abrogating the confidentiality of the counseling relationship, but courts have held that there is a compelling interest in such a situation that justifies breaching the confidential communication.

Prior to *Nally*, the most well-known counseling negligence case was *Tarasoff v. Board of Regents of the University of California.*[2] In 1969, Prosenjit Poddar, a student at the University of California at Berkeley, confided to Dr. Lawrence Moore, a psychologist at the university hospital, his intention to kill his former girlfriend, Tatiana Tarasoff. At Dr. Moore's request, the campus police briefly detained Poddar but released him when he appeared rational.

Two months later, Poddar killed Tatiana Tarasoff, and her parents sued the university, several physicians at the hospital, and several members of the university's police force. The California Supreme Court found in favor of the parents:

2. Tarasoff v. Board of Regents of the University of California, 551 P.2d 334 (S.Ct. Cal. 1976).

> When a therapist determines, or pursuant to the standards of his profession should determine, that his patient presents a serious danger of violence to another, he incurs an obligation to use reasonable care to protect the intended victim against such danger. . . . It may call for him to warn the intended victim of the danger, to notify the police, or to take whatever other steps are reasonably necessary under the circumstances.[3]

The court concluded in the specific case that the university therapists owed a legal duty of care not only to the patient (Poddar) but also to the patient's would-be victim (Tarasoff), and that the therapists' duty included not only reporting Poddar to the police but also informing Tatiana Tarasoff of the potential danger. The court also held that it was appropriate to err on the side of safety, stating that "the risk that unnecessary warnings may be given is a reasonable price to pay for the lives of possible victims that may be saved."[4]

In determining liability, the court concluded that while the therapists had a duty of care to Tatiana Tarasoff, the campus police did "not have any such special relationship to either Tatiana or to Poddar sufficient to impose upon such defendants a duty to warn respecting Poddar's violent intentions."[5] Therefore, it was the counseling professional, trained to recognize suicidal tendencies, who held primary liability in the *Tarasoff* case.

The most well-known case involving duty to a third party, *Tarasoff* presents an excellent example of the principle of *stare decisis*, or ruling precedent. In 1975, for example, John Patterson shot and killed his mother, Mollie Barnes. Patterson had been an inpatient at the Northville State Hospital, in Michigan, under a formal voluntary order. On September 2, 1975, he requested release from the hospital, and Dr. Yong-Oh Lhim, a staff psychiatrist, discharged him the following day. He stayed with relatives in Detroit until October, when he became difficult to manage, and an aunt took him to his mother, who was staying in Alabama. On November 2, 1975,

3. Ibid. at 340.
4. Ibid. at 346.
5. Ibid. at 349.

Patterson began firing a shotgun in his aunt's house, where his mother was staying. After his mother tried to talk him out of shooting again, a struggle ensued, and Patterson fired several more shots, one of which killed his mother.

Ruby Davis, Patterson's aunt and administratrix of Mollie Barnes's estate, brought suit against Dr. Lhim and the hospital, alleging that the negligent discharge of Patterson was the proximate cause of Barnes's death. The complaint also alleged that the defendants negligently failed to warn Mollie Barnes that Patterson was a danger to her safety. After a trial that lasted several days, a jury returned a verdict against Dr. Lhim and the hospital in the amount of $500,000, and the verdict was upheld by the Michigan Court of Appeals twice before finally being reversed by the state supreme court.[6]

The *Davis* court based its holding on *Tarasoff*, which they termed the leading case: "Under the common law, no one owes any duty to protect an individual who is endangered by a third person *unless* he has some special relationship with either the dangerous person or the potential victim. . . . Michigan case law supports the *Tarasoff* holding."[7]

## Danger to Unnamed Others

Danger to an *unnamed other* occurs when a counselee makes a threat to do bodily harm to a nonspecified person or persons, e.g., "I'm going to kill somebody." In this situation, there is no identifiable victim that can be warned of impending harm.

6. Davis v. Lhim, 335 N.W. 2d 481 (Mich. App. 1983). The *Davis* case was consolidated with two other psychiatric malpractice cases, and the verdict was finally reversed in 1988 when the Michigan Supreme Court determined that Dr. Lhim's action was discretionary rather than ministerial, i.e., Lhim made a reasonable decision based on his professional clinical judgment rather than neglecting to follow a treatment plan developed by someone else. Canon v. Thumudo, 422 N.W.2d 688 (S.Ct. Mich. 1988).

   As in *Nally*, while the defendants won after previously unsuccessful appeals, the case traveled through several levels of the Michigan court system and was in litigation for well over a decade.
7. Davis, 335 N.W. 2d at 486-87 (italics original).

In *Thompson v. County of Alameda*,[8] the California Supreme Court held that a duty to warn does not necessarily exist when a potential victim is not specified. "James F.," a juvenile offender confined in a county institution, made general threats that he would kill a child in his neighborhood. Within twenty-four hours of his release on temporary leave, James made good on his threat. Upholding the dismissal of a claim against the county, the court reasoned that unlike *Tarasoff*, in which there was an identifiable victim, the victim in *Thompson* was not clearly identified. The lack of a specific threat, the court said, made the threat less credible and also made warnings more difficult and less effective as a practical matter.

On the other hand, courts have ruled that even in cases where no duty to warn exists, there may be a duty to seek the commitment of a person who poses a danger to an unspecified victim. In *Currie v. United States*,[9] a federal district court granted summary judgment in favor of a Veterans Administration hospital in the case of Leonard Avery, a former patient who entered an IBM plant where he worked with a semi-automatic rifle, killed one employee, and wounded several others.

Avery, a Vietnam veteran, had been diagnosed as suffering from post-traumatic stress disorder. He had been treated on an outpatient basis at the VA hospital. In addition to his attendance at group therapy sessions, physicians prescribed anti-psychotic medications for him. During the course of his treatment, Avery admitted to carrying a gun "with thoughts of hurting anyone who would take away his property."[10] After he continued to make threats, his physicians warned both local and federal authorities, as well as IBM, of the possible danger.

Even though finding in favor of the hospital in the specific case, the court carefully differentiated between a *duty to warn* and a *duty to commit*. Noting that a duty to warn is limited to patients who have "readily identifiable victims," the court stated:

8. Thompson v. County of Alameda, 614 P.2d 728 (S.Ct. Cal. 1980).
9. Currie v. United States, 644 F.Supp. 1074 (M.D.N.C. 1986).
10. Ibid. at 1075.

> Unlike a duty to warn case, in which the therapist needs to know the identity of the victim in order to adequately act, the therapist in a duty to commit case need only know that the patient is dangerous generally in order to adequately commit him. As a practical matter, the victim's identity is irrelevant to whether the doctor can adequately act—by committing the patient, the therapist is able to protect all possible victims.
>
> The court does not believe that it is wise to limit any duty to commit according to the victim. Arguably, the patient who will kill wildly (rather than specifically identifiable victims) is the one most in need of confinement.[11]

The duty to commit may, at times, include a duty to adequately supervise a person under care. In *Sterling v. Bloom*,[12] the Idaho Supreme Court held that a probation officer owed a duty of care to motorists on the same highway as a drunk driver negligently permitted to operate a motor vehicle for recreational purposes during his probationary period.

Bloom, the codefendant along with the Idaho Department of Corrections, was sentenced to a five-year probation as a result of his third conviction for drunk driving. On June 30, 1982, driving an automobile while his blood alcohol content was .23 percent, he struck a motorcycle driven by the plaintiff, Sterling, who suffered extensive physical and mental damages and loss of work.

The court ruled that the Idaho Probation Department acted negligently in its supervision of Bloom by

> (1) allowing Bloom to drive a motor vehicle for non-employment purposes, contrary to the order of probation; (2) allowing Bloom to operate a motor vehicle without a required written permission; (3) allowing Bloom to operate an uninsured motor vehicle; (4) allowing Bloom to reside in a same building which housed a cocktail lounge and to work there as a bartender; (5) failing to require Bloom to report to his supervising probation officer on a regular basis, and failing to otherwise supervise his activities; (6) failing to revoke Bloom's probation despite previ-

11. Ibid. at 1079 (italics original).
12. Sterling v. Bloom, 723 P.2d 755 (S.Ct. Iowa 1986).

ous violations; and (7) failing to act reasonably and prudently under the circumstances despite having knowledge of Bloom's prior convictions.[13]

After enumerating the charges, the court held that "each and all of those foregoing negligent acts and omissions of the Board were proximate causes of the collision and plaintiff Maude Sterling's damages."[14]

## Danger to Nonpersons

In addition to the traditional concept of a person's being a "danger to self or others," there may also be a duty of care in the case of a counselee who is a potential danger to a property or other nonperson. Imagine a wolf going to a counselor and, referring to the Three Little Pigs, threatening, "I'm going to huff, and puff, and blow their house down." This would constitute such a danger.

John Peck, twenty-nine years old, was an outpatient of the Counseling Service of Addison County, Vermont. During the course of his therapy, he told his counselor-psychotherapist that he "wanted to get back at his father." When asked how, he replied, "I don't know, I could burn down his barn."

The next night, John set fire to his parents' barn, which was located 130 feet from their house. The barn was completely destroyed. Charles and Margaret Peck, John's parents, brought suit against the counseling service, alleging negligence on the part of the counselors in failing to take reasonable steps to protect them from the threat posed by their son.

The Vermont Supreme Court affirmed a 50 percent judgment for the Pecks, finding that they were aware of John's proclivity to violent behavior, that they knew or should have known that their actions would cause John to become angry, and that when he was angry he was capable of violent acts.[15] With regard to duty of care, the court stated:

13. Ibid. at 757.
14. Ibid.
15. Peck v. Counseling Service of Addison County, 499 A.2d 422, 427 (S.Ct. Vt. 1985).

> A mental patient's threat of serious harm to an identified victim is an appropriate circumstance under which the physician-patient privilege may be waived. This exception to the physician-patient privilege is similar to that recognized in the attorney-client relationship when a client informs an attorney of his or her intent to commit a crime.[16]

There are two significant aspects to the decision. First, the court held that the "therapist-counselor" owed a duty of care to the Pecks, even though the counselor was neither a physician nor a psychologist. Second, the court interpreted harm to a *victim* to include the Pecks' property. Therefore, a duty of care existed even though no threat was made to a person.

## A Caveat on Confidentiality

There is general agreement within both the courts and the counseling professions that the decision to break confidentiality in order to protect either the counselee or a third party should be based on sound clinical judgment. In the heat of emotion, a person may make a threat that he or she has no intention of carrying out. There is, for example, a difference between a counselee saying, "Sometimes I could just kill my (wife/husband/parent/child)," and, "I'm going to go home tonight and kill my (wife/husband/parent/child)."

The key question to ask yourself in the event that a counselee threatens violence is, "What is the chance that the person I'm counseling will actually carry out this threat?" The degree of responsibility you will be held to in a court of law will generally be the clinical judgment you exhibit within the scope of training and experience for your position (e.g., pastor, professional counselor, lay counselor). Another way of putting it is that the court will look at what the *average prudent person* in your position would do.

Counseling professionals also agree that any decision to communicate the potential of violence to someone outside the counseling relationship should be discussed with the

16. Ibid. at 426.

counselee *prior* to discussing the matter with the police, warning an intended victim, or speaking with other involved parties. This may not be prudent in all situations, but it should be attempted whenever possible.

Finally, it is important for counselors to consider what they would do in a potentially violent situation *before* such a situation occurs and to ensure that they will be protected under the law if there is the need to break the confidentiality of the counseling relationship. To take action hastily and without being aware of your legal standing could result in the action backfiring on you as a counselor.

In *Hopewell v. Adibempe*, for example, a patient told her psychiatrist that she would "blow up and hurt somebody very seriously if the harassment" at her job did not stop, specifically directing her anger toward her supervisor. Without informing the patient or obtaining her consent, the psychiatrist sent the following letter to the woman's personnel director:

> In the course of a psychiatric interview which took place in my office . . . the above-named reported feelings of being so enraged about her work situation that she "will blow up and hurt somebody very seriously if the harassment does not stop."
>
> This information is being relayed to you because there is a legal precedent requiring it and it is not to be taken as an estimate of the probability that the threat will be carried out. It is, however, important that the person or persons at risk be notified. In this case I believe that her immediate supervisor should know of this letter.
>
> [Stamped on the letter:] *This information has been disclosed to you from records whose confidentiality is protected by state law. State regulations prohibit you from making any further disclosures of this information without the prior consent of the person in respect to whom it pertains.*[17]

The patient sued, and the psychiatrist was held liable for breach of confidentiality. In his analysis of the case, psychiatrist James C. Beck points out several fallacies:

17. Hopewell v. Adibempe, No. GD78-82756, Civil Division, Court of Common Pleas of Allegheny County, Pennsylvania, June 1, 1981.

1. The court noted that *Tarasoff* raised the question of a duty but that in the state where the plaintiff lived the law effectively eliminated the *Tarasoff* duty by striking the balance in favor of confidentiality by passing an appropriate statute.
2. The defendant psychiatrist was held liable not for breach of a *Tarasoff* duty, which the court held did not exist in that jurisdiction, but for breach of confidentiality.
3. It appears that the psychiatrist, who concluded that the threat was not likely to be carried out, was motivated primarily by a concern to fulfill a legal obligation rather than by his clinical assessment of what may have been appropriate in the counseling situation.
4. The letter of warning was sent by regular mail, a slow and uncertain means of communicating with a potential victim, and one that did not allow the recipient an opportunity to ask questions or provide feedback. Additionally, he further slowed the communication by sending the letter to the personnel office rather than directly to the supervisor; this also resulted in a further breach of the patient's confidentiality.
5. Regardless of the motivation of the psychiatrist, the case supports the importance of gaining a counselee's informed consent, or at least discussing the proposed course of action with the counselee, before taking the action.[18]

The bottom line: There is no hard and fast rule for carrying out a potential duty of care to the counselee *or* to a third party. The law will generally find no fault with a counselor who warns a potential victim *if* the counselor acted in a prudent, responsible manner, but such a decision should be made with a great deal of care. In short, the legal ramifications of the counseling relationship are important but must not take precedence over the ethical factors and treatment considerations within the relationship.

18. James C. Beck, ed., *The Potentially Violent Patient and the Tarasoff Decision in Psychiatric Practice* (Washington, D.C.: American Psychiatric, 1985), pp. 30-31, 103-4.

## Relevance to Christian Counselors

The most important observation we can make here is that in the *Nally* case the California Supreme Court held that the pastoral counseling staff at the Grace Community Church of the Valley did not owe a duty of care to Ken Nally. Even so, they met any possible duty to him through multiple physician referrals and attempts at follow-up care.

*Nally* dealt with a danger-to-self situation. At this writing, there have been no significant cases dealing with danger to others or danger to property that have involved pastors or Christian counselors.

The California Supreme Court set the stage for current law in Christian counseling with the *Nally* decision. Likewise, every case referenced in this chapter cited the *Tarasoff* decision, in which the court held that *nonpastoral* professional counselors have a duty of care.

Two possibilities exist in terms of imposing a duty of care on Christian counselors. First, a state other than California might rule differently in a case in which the facts are similar to *Nally*. If that happens, there would be two precedents in a danger-to-self situation involving pastoral counselors: one in favor of the church, and one against the church. At that point courts in other states could rule either way in similar cases, and the question of liability on the part of religious counselors would likely reach the United States Supreme Court. Second, it is reasonable to assume that if a future case involves homicide rather than suicide, even the California Supreme Court might rule differently than they did in *Nally*.

We should not even begin to consider the ethical ramifications here in terms of differentiating danger to self from danger to others (e.g., suicide versus homicide). Nonetheless, human nature would suggest that while *Nally* remains the strongest precedent to date in regard to Christian counselors, it is a precedent that is bound to change as new cases come along that present different factual situations.

Although, for the Christian counselor, Scripture should be the ultimate treatment standard, we must conclude that

*Nally* may not be the ultimate victory for Christian counselors. We may have won the battle, but on the legal front the war is still being fought.

# 9

# Documenting the Counseling Relationship

Due to increasing litigation against churches and Christian counselors, gone are the days when formal counseling could simply take place in the context of the relationship between the counselor and client as brothers or sisters in Christ. Today, it is important to keep a written record of the counseling relationship so that, in the event of a lawsuit, the pastor or counselor will be prepared to document what took place in the counseling sessions.

Even for the lay person serving in a church's counseling ministry, simple case notes should be maintained to document what took place during counseling sessions. In addition to the legal protection these can help provide in the event of litigation, the notes serve as a constructive tool for the counseling review process as well as a helpful aid in keeping accurate track of the progress of counseling sessions.

## Guidelines for Counseling Notes

After a formal counseling session, the pastor or counselor should write a memo or case note documenting significant topics covered in the session, including troublesome areas that may have an impact on future sessions. Many counselors recommend that notes be divided into two sections: objective and subjective (sometimes called observations and impressions). The objective section should record exactly, in narrative format rather than word for word, what the counselee said, what you said, and what you observed. This section should also include any suggestions or recommendations you made, as well as any Scriptures shared. Conclusions, speculations, or subjective impressions should be avoided in this section. The subjective section should be used for your own thoughts about the session, including your impressions of the counselee, his or her problems, reasons for those problems, and any other subjective thoughts you had about the session.

The counseling case notes should be treated with maximum confidentiality and kept in a secure environment. However, they should be written in a style that assumes they could be read one day in open court or by a party outside of the counseling relationship.

In the sense that counselors should remain cognizant of their own limitations, it is also important that the case notes not reflect judgments the counselor is not trained to make. This is especially true in the area of diagnosis. For example, a lay counselor should not document a counselee as being schizophrenic or manic-depressive if the counselor has not been trained in such diagnostic matters. In the event of litigation, such a note could result in a charge of defamation against the counselor (and his or her agency or church). Likewise, in the subjective section, counselors should avoid value judgments that cannot be objectively documented in court (such as accusing someone of "moral turpitude" if he or she has been unfaithful). The best guideline: state *facts*, not *judgments.*

## Maintaining Counseling Records

Assuming that your records are not subject to open reading due to subpoena (court order), it is important to determine how the case notes, and any other records pertaining to the counseling relationship, should be maintained. If you are a pastor or professional counselor, it is likely that your case notes will be typed by a secretary or clerical person. If this is the case, the secretary is bound by the same degree of confidentiality as you, the counselor. If the secretary types the notes on a computer or word processor and the computer is available for use by other persons, it is essential that the documents be erased from the computer disk after printing.

Counseling agencies should maintain their client records, including case notes, in locked files that are not accessible to other clients or to non-professional staff (such as office janitorial staff that may be have access to the counseling center after hours). Churches sometimes present a special problem, since smaller churches often do not have the secure conditions that ensure files will remain confidential. In this case, the files should be maintained in the parsonage or pastor's home, again in such a manner as to prevent access by persons outside the counseling relationship. In a church situation, the confidentiality of counseling notes should include preventing access by anyone outside of the counseling relationship, including other persons in authority such as elders and deacons, as well as support staff or volunteers.

Here, of course, we have an intrinsic conflict between scriptural admonitions and the principles of counseling law. Christians are admonished to "bear one another's burdens, and thus fulfill the law of Christ" (Galatians 6:2). We should "encourage one another, and build up one another" (1 Thessalonians 5:11), and confess sins "to one another and pray for one another" (James 5:16). We are family, for "even as the body is one and yet has many members, and all the members of the body, though they are many, are one body, so also is Christ" (1 Corinthians 12:12). The Bible says that if one person has a problem, it should be shared with others, and the others should pray for a resolution to the problem.

However, even in the church, where we are admonished to have pure hearts, we often end up with big mouths. In the words of James, "the tongue is a small part of the body, and yet it boasts of great things. Behold, how great a forest is set aflame by such a small fire" (James 3:5). Even at Thessalonica, Paul had to write to the church, "we hear that some among you are leading an undisciplined life, doing no work at all, but acting like busybodies" (2 Thessalonians 3:11).

I haven't seen a church yet in which a person's problems, if known, are not subject to gossip. In addition to our moral failure in this area, the release of confidential information through the nonsecure maintenance of counseling notes can result in litigation based on invasion of privacy (defined legally, in this case, as the making public of private facts).

Except in a church discipline situation in which the guidelines of Matthew 18:15-17 have been carefully followed (see chapter 10), or a case where the person being counseled has specifically requested or consented to the release of information obtained in the counseling relationship, the content of the counseling sessions and the counseling notes should remain confidential.

## A Matter of Accountability

One exception to the above guidelines for the maintenance of case notes or the content of counseling sessions is in the realm of church-based counseling. In many churches, counselors (whether lay or professional, paid or unpaid) act in a capacity in which they assist the senior pastor with the ministry of the church. (Another way of putting it is that in a church environment, the counselor serves as an extension of the pastor.) In addition to church staff being accountable to the pastor, the pastor is responsible for the entire ministry of the church. Therefore, significant events in a counseling relationship should be shared with the pastor, who is as bound by the confidentiality privilege as the counselor.

Likewise, in a church situation in which the counselor may be functioning in an office used by others when counseling sessions are not taking place, the pastor should be entrusted with the case notes so they can be stored in a secured place with limited access. The bottom line is that all steps should be taken to ensure that the notes cannot be accessed by those outside the counseling relationship.

In large churches with several pastors, the counseling responsibilities may be coordinated by a minister of counseling (that is, a pastor serving as head of the church's counseling ministry). In this case, that pastor would be the key person to coordinate the secure storage of case notes.

## Moving On to Greener Pastures

In many churches, pastors serve for only three to five years before moving on to another church or ministry. In large churches, there will be a continuity in the counseling function based on the presence of a minister of counseling or several counselors on the church staff. In this case, the counseling notes should be maintained by the church, which holds ultimate liability for the counseling relationship under the *respondeat superior* doctrine.

In smaller churches, however, where the pastor is often the only paid employee, the counseling notes should remain the property of the pastor, *even upon leaving the church.* Due to the close-knit nature of smaller congregations, there is no guarantee that upon a pastor's departure the notes will remain confidential.

This is especially true if a new pastor is not hired by the church immediately after the former pastor leaves. In these situations, churches will often use a supply pastor (i.e., a temporary minister who fills in) or laypersons in a pastoral capacity until a new pastor is hired. In such a situation, if the counseling notes fall into the hands of persons outside the counseling relationship and the counseling discussions become an item of gossip, the former pastor may be found liable of invasion of privacy. Regardless of whether the counseling notes are permanently maintained by the church or by the pastor individually, the ultimate goal must be to ensure that they remain confidential.

## Destruction of Case Notes

There is no profession-wide guideline for the destruction of counseling notes, though there is general agreement that case notes should be destroyed on a regular basis. One common standard is that counseling notes be destroyed three years after the conclusion of the counseling relationship.[1]

One mandatory factor is that case notes should not be destroyed for which you have received a subpoena (order to produce the documents in a court of law) or for which you believe you might receive a subpoena in the future. Such destruction of notes could be interpreted as obstruction of justice, and you could be held in contempt of court for destroying evidence.

If you are acting as a professional counselor and your case notes are the subject of a subpoena, they *must* be subject to access by the courts. There are two possible exceptions to this: one is if you are a minister acting in a pastoral counseling role. The other exception is if you are a licensed psychologist. In these cases, your notes will be protected by the confidentiality privilege, which precludes them from being used in open court without the client's expressed consent. In any event, it is advisable to consult an attorney if you do receive a subpoena.

Even in the presence of a valid confidentiality privilege, clients involved in a lawsuit may subpoena their own counseling records. Likewise, if you are being sued by a parishioner or client for a counseling-related matter, this abrogates the confidentiality privilege for purposes of court testimony and you will be permitted to produce your own notes in court.

Finally, even if a valid confidentiality privilege exists, the records of a deceased client cannot be withheld if subpoenaed.

## Testifying in a Court of Law

As a pastor or counselor, you may also receive a subpoena to testify in a lawsuit. If you are asked in open court about information received in a pastoral capacity, the confidentiality privilege holds unless the client has granted his or her

1. This is an area in which you might consult a local attorney. Notes should be kept for as long as necessary to cover any statute of limitations that may impact the filing of a lawsuit. These statutes are determined on a state-by-state basis.

consent for the release of confidential information. Regardless of the capacity in which you are called to testify, it is advisable to consult an attorney to discuss your role in a legal proceeding and the degree to which the confidentiality privilege protects you.

Whether you are a pastor or counselor, be prepared to defend your credentials and your pastoral or counseling experience. Regardless of how legitimate your role in the litigation, the side opposed to what you have to say may attempt to discredit your testimony. This, of course, underscores the need to accurately represent your credentials in the context of the pastoral and counseling relationships at all times.

Finally, be careful about being willing to testify as an expert witness in any court proceeding. Expert witnesses are usually paid by one side (plaintiff or defendant) in a lawsuit and normally offer testimony that is positive to that side. The role of an expert witness is objective in nature, and any opinions offered should be based on the standards of a prudent practitioner in whatever capacity you are called to testify.

It will be highly unlikely that a pastor is called as an expert witness to testify on theological matters, since doctrine is not a matter for adjudication in civil courts. However, testimony dealing with neutral principles of law (such as the polity or administrative nature of a denomination) will be allowed.

Christian counselors should again be careful in terms of acting as an expert witness. Lay counselors would generally not qualify to offer expert testimony, and professional counselors should, in addition to having a graduate counseling degree, take care not to express opinions that are beyond their level of professional training and experience. As in the case of court testimony in general, persons serving as expert witnesses should be prepared to defend their credentials and experience in open court.

# 10

# Church Discipline and Invasion of Privacy

One of the most conspicuous areas in which biblical principles may conflict with civil law is that of church discipline. Compounding the legal dilemma that can entangle a church in litigation are the most common tort claims resulting from a discipline situation: invasion of privacy, outrageous conduct, and intentional infliction of emotional distress.

There is no doubt that the Bible contains guidelines designed to restore errant believers into fellowship, to bring them into repentance, and to reconcile them with the body of Christ. This is true both in the believer's own life and in his or her relationships with other Christians:

> If your brother sins, go and reprove him in private; if he listens to you, you have won your brother. But if he does not listen to you, take one or two more with you, so that by the mouth of two or three witnesses every fact may be confirmed. And if he refuses to listen to them, tell it to the church; and if he refuses to listen even to the church, let him be to you as a Gentile and a tax-gatherer. (Matthew 18:15-17)

The church discipline process has been an integral part of some denominations for centuries. These include the Mennonites, Old Order Amish, and Society of Friends. Church discipline is also practiced by non-Christian groups such as the Jehovah's Witnesses.

Biblically, the discipline process of Matthew 18:15-17 is not used with non-Christians. Even if discipline reaches the point of shunning (exclusion from the fellowship), the apostle Paul makes clear that only believers are affected:

> I wrote you in my letter not to associate with immoral people; I did not at all mean with the immoral people of this world, or with the covetous and swindlers, or with idolaters; for then you would have to go out of the world. But actually, I wrote to you not to associate with any so-called brother if he should be an immoral person, or covetous, or an idolater, or a reviler, or a drunkard, or a swindler—not even to eat with such a one. For what have I to do with judging outsiders? Do you not judge those who are within the church? But those who are outside, God judges. Remove the wicked man from yourselves. (1 Corinthians 5:9-13)

Over the past decade, there has been a renewed interest in church discipline on the part of evangelical Christians.[1] However, the increase of litigation against churches has created a legal quagmire for churches in terms of following biblical principles. The dilemma is simple: if a church sincerely believes that discipline is required in a given situation and follows the guidelines in Matthew 18:15-17, that church may be sued. And the plaintiff is likely to win. On the other hand, if the church avoids dealing with sin in a biblical manner, the fellowship is likely to break down and a schism may form within the congregation.

In the area of church discipline it may come down to a choice: follow God's will at the risk of being sued in a civil court, or play it safe and end up like the church at Laodicea—neither cold nor hot, merely lukewarm (Revelation 3:14-16). The lawsuit that may be as well known to pastors and Christian counselors as the *Nally* case is the story of Marian Guinn.

1. See, for example, Jay E. Adams, *Handbook of Church Discipline* (Grand Rapids: Zondervan, 1986); Don Baker, *Beyond Forgiveness: The Healing Touch of Church Discipline* (Portland: Multnomah, 1984); and J. Carl Laney, *A Guide to Church Discipline* (Minneapolis: Bethany House, 1985).

## Paying the Dues of Discipline

Marian Guinn, a divorced mother of two, moved with her children to the town of Collinsville, Oklahoma, in 1974. A small town of about 3,500, Collinsville is located up the road from Tulsa in the middle of the Oklahoma Bible belt.

Marian joined the Church of Christ of Collinsville, where she became an integral part of the congregation. The Church of Christ is an autonomous church operating under a congregational form of government, the most conservative branch of a denominational fellowship that includes the Disciples of Christ and the Christian Church. Following the teachings of nineteenth-century theologians Thomas and Alexander Campbell, the Church of Christ is well known for believing in the doctrine of baptismal regeneration and for not using musical instruments in their worship services.

The Collinsville congregation extended both fellowship and aid to Marian; they helped her find a job, bought her a used car, and babysat her children while she studied for her high school equivalency diploma. After graduation, Marian continued with her education and obtained a nursing degree from the local community college. At that point, she accepted a job in Tulsa, which caused her to stop attending Sunday worship services at the church on a regular basis.[2]

In 1980, the elders of the church learned that Marian was having an affair with the former mayor of Collinsville, Pat Sharp. When the elders, pursuant to their doctrinal responsibility, which required them as church leaders to monitor the congregation members' actions and to discuss problems with those having trouble, confronted Marian with allegations of the affair, she admitted its truthfulness.

The elders met with Marian three times over the course of a year, finally advising her that "if she did not appear before the congregation and repent of her fornication, the members would withdraw fellowship from her."[3] On September 21, 1981, they confirmed their warning by letter:

2. Christopher S. Heroux, "When Fundamental Rights Collide: Guinn v. Collinsville Church of Christ," *Tulsa Law Journal* (1985): 158.
3. Guinn v. Church of Christ of Collinsville, 775 P.2d 766, 768 (S.Ct. Okla. 1989).

Dear Sister Marian:

> It is with tremendous concern for your soul and the welfare of the Lord's church that we exhort you to consider the impact of the results of the course you have elected to pursue. We have and will continue to follow the instructions set forth in the Scriptures in dealing with matters of church discipline. The Lord set forth the procedure in Matthew 18:15-17. We have confronted you personally. . . . However to date you have not responded, so you leave us no alternative but to "tell it to the church." . . . It is the prayerful desire of the entire body of Christ that you correct this serious matter and avert the "withdrawing of fellowship" of the saints.[4]

On September 25, Marian responded that the matter was "none of their business" and further wrote to the church:

> I do not want my name mentioned before the church except to tell them I withdraw my membership immediately. I have never accepted your doctrine and never will. Anything I told was in confidence and not meant for anyone else to hear. You have no right to get up and say anything against me in church. . . . I have no choice but to attend another church, another denomination where men do not set themselves up as judges for God. He does his own judging.[5]

The following Sunday, the elders read their September 21st letter to the congregation and urged the members of the church to contact Marian and encourage her to repent and return to the church. They also told the congregation that, should their attempts fail, the Scriptures that Marian had violated would be read aloud at the church's service the following week.[6]

Marian met with one of the elders the following week and reiterated her withdrawal from membership. The elder responded that withdrawing membership from the Church of Christ was doctrinally impossible and could not halt the ac-

4. Quoted in Lynn Buzzard, "Scarlet Letter Lawsuits: Private Affairs and Public Judgments," *Campbell Law Review* 10 (1987): 3.
5. Quoted in ibid.
6. Guinn, 775 P.2d at 769.

tion against her from being carried out. According to the Church of Christ, one can be born into a family but cannot truly withdraw from it. Since the church views its members as a family, one can voluntarily join the congregation but cannot then withdraw from membership.

The following week, the Scriptures Marian violated were read to the congregation, and she was publicly branded a fornicator. In addition to the Collinsville church, information about Marian's transgressions was sent to four other Church of Christ congregations to be read aloud during the services. Needless to say, Marian sued.

## Taking the Church to Court

Marian first sued the church for defamation of character.[7] Defamation, which is defined as the spreading of false rumors about a person, normally takes the form of libel or slander, depending upon whether written or verbal. There was just one problem: the fact that Marian was involved in an adulterous relationship was true. Since truth is the ultimate defense to a charge of defamation, Marian then amended her complaint.

In the amended suit, she charged the church and its three elders individually with two counts of invasion of privacy along with intentional infliction of emotional distress. And, in a jury trial in the District Court of Tulsa County, she won. The jury found the Church of Christ of Collinsville guilty of three causes of action and filed the following verdict forms:

1. *Publication of private facts*: $205,000 actual damages and $185,000 punitive damages.
2. *Intrusion upon seclusion*: $114,000 actual damages and $120,000 punitive damages.
3. *Intentional infliction of emotional distress*: $122,000 actual damages and $81,000 punitive damages.[8]

7. Theodore S. Danchi, "Church Discipline on Trial: Religious Freedom versus Individual Privacy," *Valparaiso University Law Review* 21 (1987): 413.
8. Guinn, 775 P.2d at 785.

The parties to the case had stipulated that Marian could recover only the highest amount awarded her for any of the three counts.[9] Therefore, she was effectively awarded the actual and punitive damages for the first count, or a total of $390,000. On top of the award, the trial court added $44,737 in prejudgment interest, bringing the total judgment against the church to $434,737—almost half a million dollars.

On appeal, the Oklahoma Supreme Court ruled that although the church had the right to discipline Marian, that right was abrogated when she withdrew from membership. The court, therefore, reversed the judgment of the trial court and the case was remanded back to the lower court for a recalculation of the award.

## THE IMPLICATIONS OF THE GUINN CASE

Among other things, the Oklahoma Supreme Court held the following:

> 1. The disciplinary actions taken by the elders against Marian Guinn before she withdrew her membership from the church were constitutionally protected, as they did not constitute a threat to safety, peace, or order.[10]
>
> 2. When Marian withdrew from membership, thereby withdrawing her consent to participate in a spiritual relationship in which she had implicitly agreed to submit to ecclesiastical supervision, the disciplinary actions taken against her by the elders no longer had First Amendment protection.[11]
>
> 3. After Marian withdrew from membership, the elders were neither absolutely nor conditionally privileged to publicize private facts about her life.[12]

Churches have a firm right to discipline an errant member. Marian Guinn was aware of this, since during the five-year period in which she was a member of the church, she had

9. Ibid. at 786.
10. Ibid. at 774.
11. Ibid. at 777.
12. Ibid. at 783.

witnessed at least one such disciplinary proceeding in which fellowship was withdrawn.[13]

In *Watson v. Jones*, an early church-state case, the United States Supreme Court held:

> The right to organize voluntary religious associations to assist in the expression and dissemination of any religious doctrine, and to create tribunals for the decision of controverted questions of faith within the association, and for the ecclesiastical government of all the individual members, congregations, and officers within the general association, is unquestioned. All who unite themselves to such a body do so with an implied consent to this government, and are bound to submit to it.[14]

Whether Marian was in doctrinal error was not a matter for the court to decide. A multitude of cases beginning with *Watson* determined that doctrinal matters were beyond the purview of civil adjudication:

> In these matters of religious doctrine, discipline, and church order, who is to be the judge? Who had the right to say conclusively, in case of controversy, that one or the other party [to a religious dispute] has departed from the doctrines of the church? Who shall determine upon the validity of an act or judgment of a church court; upon the status of a member or an officer?[15]

There was just one problem with the *Guinn* case: public disciplinary action was taken against Marian *after* she withdrew from membership in the church. At that point, according to the court, the church no longer had the right to invoke discipline against her.

## What Constitutes Invasion of Privacy?

A recent survey by *The National Law Journal* indicated that 73 percent of Americans believe the Constitution guar-

13. Ibid. at 768.
14. Watson v. Jones, 80 U.S. (13 Wall.) 679, 728-29 (1872).
15. Ibid. at 679-80.

antees a right to privacy, and 51 percent believe that the privacy right is explicitly enumerated in the Constitution.[16] Contrary to the popular belief, the concept of a constitutional right to privacy is a fairly recent development.

The threshold case regarding the right to privacy is *Griswold v. Connecticut*,[17] decided by the United States Supreme Court in 1965. In that case, the Court ruled that the use of contraceptive devices was a private matter not open to state interference and struck down a Connecticut law against the sale or use of contraceptives.

Eight years later, the Court reaffirmed the right to privacy in *Roe v. Wade*,[18] which determined that the right to privacy extends to the physician-patient relationship, even in the realm of abortion. As much as *Roe* is considered to be an abortion-oriented decision per se, it's also a seminal case dealing with the right to privacy.[19]

As a tort claim recognized in most states, invasion of privacy may take one of four forms: (1) intrusion upon a person's seclusion or solitude or into his or her private affairs; (2) public disclosure of embarrassing private facts about a person; (3) publicity that places a person in a false light in the public eye; and (4) appropriation of a person's name or likeness.[20] Marian Guinn successfully sued the Collinsville Church of Christ for violating the first two principles of the invasion of privacy tort.

To some degree, public figures are immune from protection based on invasion of privacy claims; the fact that they are public figures makes their lives more open to scrutiny.[21] However, the average church member or counseling client is not a public figure.

16. Marcia Coyle, "How Americans View High Court," *The National Law Journal*, 26 February 1990, p. 36.
17. Griswold v. Connecticut, 381 U.S. 479 (1965).
18. Roe v. Wade, 410 U.S. 113 (1973).
19. For an excellent treatment of how judicial activism has contributed to the concept of a constitutional right to privacy, see Robert H. Bork, *The Tempting of America: The Political Seduction of the Law* (New York: The Free Press, 1990), pp. 110-26.
20. *Restatement (Second) of Torts*, sec. 652B (1977).
21. This principle can be seen in operation with regard to politicians such as Richard Nixon and Gary Hart, not to mention prominent religious figures such as Jim Bakker and Jimmy Swaggart.

In the realm of counseling, however, even public figures would be able to sue successfully for invasion of privacy if confidential facts revealed in a counseling session were made public. A key factor here is that, if the person has a reasonable expectation of privacy, the counselor is bound by confidentiality.

Also for counselors, a common fallacy is to utilize a current client or counselee's personal situation as an illustration when teaching or lecturing. This is especially the case for pastoral counselors, who often use their congregants' problems in the context of a sermon illustration. Not only can this be detrimental in terms of creating a chilling effect in the counseling relationship, there can be severe legal repercussions if the counselee realizes that the illustration being used is about him or her (or, worse, if others in the congregation recognize the identity of the subject of the illustration), and this could result in a successful lawsuit for invasion of privacy. Therefore, it is recommended that as a pastor or counselor, you never use a current case, nor a situation involving a person in your current congregation or ministry, as a sermon or lecture illustration. By taking care that the illustrations you use are always from a source other than your current work, you can protect yourself from a lawsuit based on invasion of privacy.

## Avoiding Church Discipline Lawsuits

Based on *Watson v. Jones* and subsequent cases, the right of a church to discipline its members is firmly grounded in law. A key to this right, however, is that members coming into the church should be informed of the church's policies regarding disciplinary matters. Thus, their implied consent to the procedures will be given in an informed manner. This brings us back to the doctrine of informed consent discussed in chapter 7.

The phrase *informed consent* is commonly used with regard to medical treatment; before a person goes into an operating room for a surgical procedure, a medical professional will review the nature of the operation, the probability of success, and the risks involved, after which the patient signs a form acknowledging that he or she understands the procedure and has given his or her informed consent. In historical context, the term is usually used with regard to procedures that are invasive, such as surgical or diagnostic procedures that invade a person's body.

In the context of church membership, informed consent can also be used to signify that a person understands the policies of a church upon applying for membership. The most common way to ensure a potential member's understanding of the church's beliefs, doctrines, polity, and disciplinary procedures is to provide them with a copy of the church's governing documents, such as a constitution or bylaws.

Based on the Oklahoma Supreme Court's opinion in *Guinn*, it would appear that a church can discipline a person who withdraws from the membership roll *if* such a policy is specified in the church's governing documents or otherwise communicated to a person *before* he or she accepts membership. The court wrote that the right of a person to withdraw his or her consent to submit to disciplinary procedures "is constitutionally unqualified; its relinquishment would have required a knowing and intelligent waiver."[22] Keep in mind, however, that the *Guinn* ruling is binding only in the state of Oklahoma and may not be followed in other states.

Likewise, the waiver of a person's right to be free from disciplinary action if he or she withdraws from a congregation should be documented by a written, signed waiver. Even if a church were to implement the use of such a form, it is highly likely that it would create a chilling effect on gaining new members (not to mention retaining current members).

Another factor is that, if a church's constitution or bylaws do not already include a clause regarding church discipline, adding such a policy is easier said than done. The best time to include such a clause is during the initial writing of the documents; in addition to constitutional amendments often involving a lengthy implementation process, it's likely that a church's congregation will resist the addition of a discipline clause if there hasn't been one in the past. Not surpris-

22. Guinn, 775 P.2d at 775.

ingly, part of this is due to human nature; we recognize that 1 Corinthians 6:1-7 precludes Christians from suing other Christians, but we don't want to give up our right to do so.

Church discipline, then, presents us with a potential win-lose situation. If we follow scriptural guidelines, we can be sued. If we don't, we end up compromising the mission of the church.

The proper action may be painful for the church, but the church should be faithful to God's Word even at the risk of being sued. The apostle Peter wrote, "Therefore, let those also who suffer according to the will of God entrust their souls to a faithful Creator in doing what is right" (1 Peter 4:19). At the same time, Jesus said not to fear "what you are about to suffer. Behold, the devil is about to cast some of you into prison [or, perhaps, into court], that you may be tested, and you will have tribulation ten days [the length of an average legal proceeding, perhaps?]. Be faithful until death, and I will give you the crown of life" (Revelation 2:10).

Jesus makes the cost of faithfulness clear: "Whoever does not carry his own cross and come after me cannot be my disciple. . . . What king, when he sets out to meet another king in battle, will not first sit down and take counsel whether he is strong enough with ten thousand men to encounter the one coming against him with twenty thousand? Or else, while the other is still far away, he sends a delegation and asks terms of peace" (Luke 14:27, 31-32).

Churches should take all steps possible to seek reconciliation with an errant member but should do so without compromising God's explicit Word. If prayer were ever needed, this is perhaps the legal area in which it is needed the most.[23]

## A FINAL WORD ON INVASION OF PRIVACY: AIDS

One final area that should be addressed under the rubric of invasion of privacy is that of Acquired Immune Deficiency Syndrome (AIDS). AIDS has spread to such a degree that few

23. For a more comprehensive discussion of church discipline and the *Guinn* case, see Lynn R. Buzzard and Thomas S. Brandon, Jr., *Church Discipline and the Courts* (Wheaton, Ill.: Tyndale, 1987).

churches will be able to avoid confronting the issue. To date, the majority of AIDS cases are in the gay community. Many homosexuals who were brought up in Bible-believing churches, especially in small towns, gravitated toward larger cities where they could engage in what secular sources call an "alternative lifestyle" with less fear of reprisal. As AIDS takes its toll, many urban homosexuals are going back to their roots, very often going home to die in the smaller cities and towns in which they were born.

Dealing with AIDS is a painful task and requires too extensive a treatment for the context of this volume. Churches are just beginning to formulate policies with regard to members who test HIV-positive or manifest the actual disease in the form of AIDS or AIDS-Related Complex (ARC). Certainly, the best time to consider an AIDS policy is before the need arises.[24]

From the counseling perspective, the most likely scenario is that you may be called on to counsel a person who has tested HIV-positive or perhaps has already been diagnosed as having AIDS. Take the hypothetical case of Jim Smith, a recent resident of the "gay ghetto" in a large city. Jim has been diagnosed with AIDS and has moved back to his small town, where he is living with his parents until the disease takes its toll and he dies. At the moment, Jim appears to be in moderately good health. He has not lost much weight, his face does not bear the signs of a body wasting away, and he does not manifest symptoms of Kaposi's sarcoma, the skin cancer that often accompanies AIDS and results in purple lesions on the body.

Jim wants to return to the fellowship of the body of Christ, and his church has welcomed him with open arms. There's just one problem: as much as Jim realizes that he must give up the gay lifestyle, he still craves the dangerous thrill of having sex with other men despite his disease. He

24. For an overview of how churches have dealt with the AIDS crisis, see William E. Amos, Jr., "When AIDS Comes to Church," *Leadership*, Fall 1989, pp. 66-73; Randy Frame, "AIDS: Coming to a Church Near You," *Christianity Today*, 18 June 1990, pp. 50-52; and Steve Lawson, "The AIDS Debate: An Interview with C. Everett Koop," *Charisma & Christian Life*, June 1989, pp. 72-77.

confides to his counselor that several evenings a week he "cruises" the local highways and parks, where he meets men and has sex with them. His sexual practices do not include the use of a condom and are considered unsafe by the medical profession.

By nature, Jim is obviously spreading the AIDS virus to others. In counseling terms, he is creating a "danger to unnamed others" (see chapter 8), and it would appear to be appropriate for the counselor to attempt to take steps to prevent Jim from passing AIDS to other persons. Legally, however, it is not that simple. There have been few cases in which the AIDS issue has been tested in court. Those that have been heard have dealt primarily with employment issues and have been decided in favor of the AIDS carrier.[25]

Even in terms of a potential duty of care to other persons, it is likely that warning possible victims of Jim's activities will be considered a breach of confidentiality. Compounding this is the logistical factor that since Jim tends to pick up strangers for sex, there is no known victim to warn. Short of tattooing Jim's forehead identifying him as an AIDS patient (a solution I hope no one would support) or placing him in a

25. The only case that has reached the United States Supreme Court thus far with any relevance to AIDS has been *Board of Education of Nassau County v. Arline*, 107 S.Ct. 1123 (1987). In this case, the Court held that a woman suffering from infectious tuberculosis qualified as a disabled person under Sec. 504 of the Rehabilitation Act of 1973 and had the same right to work as a person with any other disability. The Court's ruling was extended by a federal appeals court to include AIDS in *Chalk v. U.S. District Court*, 840 F.2d 701 (9th Cir. 1988), in which it was held that a person with AIDS (the manifest disease, not just a carrier of the HIV virus) is a protectable handicapped person, thus restoring him to the teaching post he held prior to his diagnosis.

In 1990 Congress passed the Americans with Disabilities Act, which extends Sec. 504's provisions to those who work in the private sector. Whether this will include churches is unknown at this time, but the issue is likely to be tested in court in the future. Another issue likely to be tested in courts is tort liability in the area of sexual transmission of AIDS. In a first-of-its-kind suit filed in July 1990 in Florida, John Hill filed suit against his former lover, Marion L. Miller, for allegedly giving him AIDS. Both men had allegedly committed to a monogamous relationship, and Miller told Hill that he was free of any transmissible diseases. (See Victoria Slind-Flor, "At the Limits: Major AIDS Cases Have Been Teaching Old Law New Tricks," *The National Law Journal*, 27 August 1990, p. 31.) However, the transmission of AIDS is not limited to homosexuals, and a similar issue may present itself in a Christian counseling situation involving a married couple in which one partner contracts AIDS outside of the marital relationship and transmits it to his or her spouse.

quarantine situation (which, again, most people would not support), there is no way to exercise a duty of care with regard to possible victims.

Society in general is having trouble dealing with the privacy rights of the individual versus the rights of the larger population vis-a-vis AIDS. At the moment, there are no significant rulings dealing with AIDS and the right to privacy, especially with regard to confidentiality in the counseling relationship. However, future cases are likely to address this issue as the incidence of AIDS increases.

# 11

# Child Abuse Reporting: An Ethical Dilemma

According to recent FBI statistics, one in five girls and one in seven boys will be sexually assaulted before their eighteenth birthday. In 80 percent of child sexual abuse cases, the offender will be someone the child knows.[1] All fifty states plus the District of Columbia and the Virgin Islands have enacted child abuse reporting statutes that provide for the identification and investigation of suspected child abuse and the possible intervention where abuse is proved. At the same time, forty-eight states, the District of Columbia, and the Virgin Islands also have statutes granting a confidentiality privilege to communications between pastors and penitents when the clergyman is acting in his professional capacity, in confidence, and for spiritual purposes.[2]

In most states, an intrinsic conflict exists between the pastor's duty to maintain the confidentiality of the parishioner in the course of penitential counseling and the obligation to report suspected child abuse. Some states have resolved this dilemma, at least on its face, by enacting statutes that specifically exempt clergy from child sexual abuse reporting

1. *The Philadelphia Inquirer*, 8 April 1990, p. 3-H.
2. William N. Ivers, "When Must a Priest Report Under a Child Abuse Reporting Statute? Resolution to the Priest's Conflicting Duties," *Valparaiso University Law Review* 21 (1987): 431-32.

requirements. These states include Washington, California, Kansas, New York, and Ohio.[3]

## Confidentiality and Child Abuse Reporting Laws

Pennsylvania provides an excellent comparative example of a state with several statutes that impact pastoral counselors in terms of both privileged communications and child abuse reporting requirements.[4] This state defines child abuse as

> serious physical or mental injury which is not explained by the available medical history as being accidental, or sexual abuse or sexual exploitation, or serious physical neglect, of a child under 18 years of age, if the injury, abuse or neglect has been caused by the acts or omissions of the child's parents or by a person responsible for the child's welfare, or any individual residing in the same home as the child, or a paramour of the child's parent.[5]

The same statute defining child abuse specifically exempts cases in which the child is in good faith being furnished treatment by spiritual means through prayer alone or is not provided specified medical treatment on the basis of religious belief.[6]

Most professional treatment personnel are required to report proved or suspected cases of child abuse, to the extent that the reporting requirement abrogates the confidentiality privilege. In Pennsylvania, persons required to report abuse include the following:

> Any licensed physician, medical examiner, coroner, funeral director, dentist, osteopath, optometrist, chiropractor, podia-

3. Lee W. Carlson, *Child Sexual Abuse: A Handbook for Clergy and Church Members* (Valley Forge, Pa.: Judson, 1988), p. 38.
4. For the text of Pennsylvania's confidentiality statute for pastors, see chapter 7, text for note 3.
5. 11 Pennsylvania Statutes (P.S.) 2203 (1985).
6. Ibid. Exemptions include treatment by a Christian Science practitioner or the withholding of certain treatments for a Jehovah's Witness. With an increasing amount of litigation arising in this area, however, many states are leaning toward the removal of this exemption for cases involving children.

> trist, intern, registered nurse, licensed practical nurse, hospital personnel engaged in the admission, examination, care or treatment of persons, a Christian Science practitioner, school administrator, school teacher, school nurse, social services worker, day care center worker or any other child care or foster care worker, mental health professional, peace officer or law enforcement official. The privileged communication between any professional person required to report and his patient or client shall not apply to situations involving child abuse and shall not constitute grounds for failure to report as required by this act.[7]

The statute goes on to state, "In addition to those persons and officials required to report suspected child abuse, any person may make such a report if that person has reasonable cause to suspect that a child is an abused child."[8] Therefore, while there is a specific list of professionals who are *required* to report cases of child abuse, any other person *may* report such cases. Due to the compelling interest in protecting children, persons who report cases of suspected abuse in good faith are immune from any liability, civil or criminal, that may result from a report that proves false.[9]

In the above list of persons required to report child abuse, one occupational classification is glaringly absent: clergy. The clergy exemption is, in fact, specifically enumerated in terms of court testimony in abuse cases:

> Except for privileged communications between a lawyer and his client and between a minister and his penitent, any privilege of confidential communication between husband and wife or between any professional person, including but not limited to physicians, psychologists, counselors, employees of hospitals, clinics, day care centers, and schools and their patients or clients, shall not constitute grounds for excluding evidence at any proceeding regarding child abuse or the cause thereof.[10]

7. 11 P.S. 2204(c) (1987). Reporting statutes vary from state to state; pastors are advised to contact an attorney or their local Children and Youth Services bureau to determine reporting statutes for their state.
8. 11 P.S. 2205 (1975).
9. 11 P.S. 2211 (1985).
10. 11 P.S. 2222(2) (1975).

## Additional Reporting Considerations

The key to understanding the clergy exemption to the reporting requirement is in the minister-*penitent* relationship. For example, if a man goes to his pastor and confesses that he has sexually abused his child, that he is repentant and wants to "get right with God," the abuse does not have to be reported. Two conditions exist that protect the confidentiality of the communication: first, the minister has been approached in a pastoral role, and second, the confession is penitential in nature.

A legal dilemma is faced when the minister is not acting in a pastoral capacity or when the counseling is not penitential. In Alabama, for example, a man confessed the murder of his girlfriend to a local pastor. The minister reported the man to the police, and the man's lawyer attempted to have the evidence barred from trial based on the priest-penitent privilege. The court decided to admit the evidence, ruling that when the man made the confession at the minister's home he was seeking refuge from the police and was not making a penitential confession.[11]

In a recent California case involving the South Bay Pentecostal Church in Chula Vista, a young girl attending the South Bay Christian Academy approached two pastors in the school and informed them that she was being sexually molested by her stepfather, who had been a lay preacher at the church. The pastors did not report the abuse and were charged with violating California's reporting statute. The California Superior Court upheld a municipal court decision refusing to dismiss charges against the ministers, ruling that when they heard the girl's confession they were acting as administrators of the Christian Academy and, as such, "child care custodians." The pastors should have reported the abuse since (1) they were not acting in a penitential counseling role, and (2) they learned about the abuse from the victim rather than from a repentant offender.[12]

11. Lucy v. State, 443 So.2d 1335 (Crim. App. Ala. 1983).
12. People v. Hodges, No. 614153 (Cal. App. Dept. Super. Ct. 1989).

It is also important to note that those states that exempt clergy from mandatory child abuse reporting limit the exemption to clergy acting in a pastoral capacity. Professional Christian counselors who are not acting in a pastoral capacity are considered to be "mental health professionals" and are required to report. This includes professional counseling staff at a church-based or independent Christian counseling agency, as well as ordained counselors who are not acting in a pastoral role at the time they learn of an abuse situation.

## The Clergy As Child Abusers

Another consideration is that many child abusers are also members of the clergy, often resulting in litigation against churches based on negligent hiring and supervision under the doctrine of *respondeat superior* (in which the employer is liable for the acts of the employee). For example, the media has reported more than 140 cases of priests accused of molesting children in eighteen states, and a 1985 report to the U.S. Catholic bishops estimated that diocesan payments to victims could reach $1 billion during the 1990s.[13] The situation is complicated by the fact that victims of sexual abuse will disclose their story to an average of nine people before anyone believes them.[14]

In one unique case that provides an indication of how a child sexual abuse situation can have a negative impact on the church, a Catholic priest in Camden, New Jersey, was convicted of molesting a teenage boy in his youth ministry. Shortly after his arrest in 1988, he was suspended from his youth ministry post, convicted the following month, and sentenced shortly thereafter to five years in prison. The Diocese of Camden reached an out-of-court settlement with the boy's family in the amount of $2.3 million.

The above scenario is common thus far. There is, however, a punch line that indicates the extent to which churches

13. Rorie Sherman, "Legal Spotlight on Priests Who Are Pedophiles," *The National Law Journal*, 4 April 1988, p. 28.
14. Michael E. Phillips, "Helping the Sexually Abused," *Leadership* 89 (Summer 1989): 65.

will be sued: the priest, now a convicted child molester, has sued the Camden diocese, its bishop, and a diocesean administrator for breach of contract, charging that they failed to support him "both morally and financially."[15]

## Reporting Versus Repentance: The Ethical Dilemma

Though in many states clergy are not required to report cases of child abuse when confession is made by the offender in a penitential counseling situation, there are considerations indicating that the need to report may at times override the concern for maintaining confidentiality. The first is the potential for recidivism among child abusers. One study reported that 37 percent of offenders serving time in prison for child abuse were recidivists, i.e., they had at least one prior child abuse conviction. The same study indicated a 50 percent undetected recidivism rate, i.e., cases in which the offenders had committed child sexual abuse previously without getting caught.[16]

The treatment of sexual abusers is a specialized field in which few clergy are adequately trained. Even for those persons who have a pastoral degree or a graduate degree in Christian counseling, the average Christian counseling curriculum does not include extensive study in the etiology and treatment of child abuse or sexual abuse. Due to the high recidivism rate in child sexual abusers, it is unlikely that the pastor or Christian counselor will be successful in treating an offender, even in an ongoing counseling relationship.

It is a sad fact that most professionals who are trained to treat child abusers tend to practice in the secular counseling area. Therefore, pastors should seek to be trained in the issues involved in counseling child abusers within the fellowship and should consider hiring or networking with Christian counselors who have dealt with both offenders and victims of

15. "Priest, Convicted of Molesting Teen, Sues Diocese of Camden," *The Philadelphia Inquirer*, 8 May 1990, p. 2-B.
16. A. Nicholas Groth, Robert E. Longo, and J. Bradley McFadin, "Undetected Recidivism Among Rapists and Child Molesters," *Crime & Delinquency* 28 (1982): 452-54.

sexual abuse. The issue is too urgent to ignore and too important for the church to leave to secular professionals.

A further dilemma is faced when examining the scriptural basis for forgiveness and reconciliation. In discussing the issue of unrighteousness versus sanctification and justification, Paul lists a litany of persons who will not inherit the kingdom of God, then observes, "And such *were* some of you; but you were washed, but you were sanctified, but you were justified in the name of the Lord Jesus Christ, and in the Spirit of our God" (1 Corinthians 6:11; italics added).

Even if the offender professes Christianity and is caught in the sin of child sexual abuse, Scripture mandates a spirit of repentance on the part of the offender *and* forgiveness on the part of the church (Matthew 18:15). The sin, once repented of, is in the past, and the offender is to be reconciled to the church (2 Corinthians 5:17-18).

God, it seems, is able to forgive sin faster than man (Psalms 32:5; 103:12). The stigma of child abuse, however, is such that reporting its occurrence is often a guarantee of a mandatory prison sentence for the offender. It is interesting that even in the prison environment, in which the commission of crimes is a norm, the sexual abuse of a child is looked upon as a heinous crime by most convicts. An offender who is convicted of child abuse and sentenced to a prison term is therefore likely to become a victim himself of possible murder, emasculation, or prison rape.

(This observation should not be taken as an attempt to minimize the trauma the abused child goes through, which normally requires ongoing counseling for an extended period. Likewise, the parents and family of the victim often require counseling. A common after-effect of child abuse is the breakup of the family structure, especially when the offender is a parent or relative of the victim.)

The reporting dilemma, then, can be delineated by the conflict between knowing that God can heal an offender of the sin of child abuse, contrasted with the possibility that the person is likely to commit future abuse if the act goes unreported. In those cases in which a pastor or church staff member is the abuser, a church or denomination may or may not experience negative legal impact depending upon whether the church had previous knowledge of the person's history of abuse.

In one California case, a Baptist Sunday school teacher had a two-year sexual relationship with a male second grader. Holding that the church was not liable for the teacher's conduct, the court used a twofold test to determine whether the teacher's conduct was within the realm of *respondeat superior*: whether the act performed was required or incidental to the employee's duties, and whether the employee's misconduct could reasonably be foreseen by the employer. The court concluded that the teacher's acts were not within the scope of his employment as a Sunday school teacher.[17]

The opposite result was reached in the state of Washington. A priest in the Lafayette, Louisiana, diocese was suspended from his priestly duties for sexual misconduct with minors and obtained treatment at the House of Affirmation in Massachusetts. Upon discharge, he was placed under the supervision of the Lafayette diocese and later transferred to Washington state, where he was employed in a medical center's adolescent unit and committed abuse again. In a pretrial hearing, the Washington Appeals Court stated with respect to negligent supervision that the employer may be held liable for acts beyond the scope of the priest's employment because the employer had prior knowledge of the employee's tendencies.[18]

Acts of marital infidelity on the part of both church members and clergy can often be dealt with within a pastoral counseling relationship or a church fellowship and can result in both healing and reconciliation. The roots of the adultery, however, are often within the marriage or family relationship. Christian counseling can bring out the underlying factors that resulted in the act of infidelity and then begin to effect a resolution of the problem. Child abuse and sexual abuse, unfortunately, have much deeper causative factors,

17. Jeffrey Scott E. v. Central Baptist Church, 197 Cal. App. 3d (1988).
18. John Does 1-9 v. Compcare, Inc., 763 P.2d 1237 (Wash. App. 1988).

and most Christian counselors are not trained in their analysis or treatment.

Until the church can begin to deal with child abusers with a secure assurance that incidents of recidivism will not occur, perhaps the best action for pastors to take is to report the abuse, even at the expense of abrogating the confidentiality privilege. The price is high and could result in a chilling effect within the counseling relationship. However, the price of ongoing sexual abuse on the victim is even higher, and the risk of allowing an abuse situation to continue is too great.

# 12

# Counseling and Medical Issues

Death and dying have always been a part of human life, and comforting the grieving has always played a part in the pastoral ministry. Yet as we approach the twenty-first century, grief counseling will be pushed aside, in part, to share space with the increasing role of pastors and Christian counselors in medical treatment issues.

With an increased emphasis on wellness and preventive medicine, people are remaining healthier and living longer than ever before. Death, when it occurs, is no longer as sudden as it once was; long-term illness requiring treatment decisions by patients and family members is gaining steady ground. Technological advances that result in the decrease of morbidity or mortality[1] for one disease often result in an increase for another. Since 1968, for example, the death rate from both heart disease and stroke has declined for persons seventy-five to seventy-nine years of age, while the death rate from cancer for the same age group has increased. These trends are expected to continue through the year 2000 and beyond.[2]

On top of breakthroughs in the treatment of disease, technology has created new issues that will demand the at-

1. *Morbidity* refers to statistical data regarding the occurrence of disease, and *mortality* deals with statistics regarding death as a result of disease.
2. Karen Davis and Diane Rowland, *Medicare Policy: New Directions for Health and Long-Term Care* (Baltimore: The Johns Hopkins University Press, 1986), pp. 14-15.

tention not only of ethicists and theologians but of pastors at the level of the local church. These include *in vitro* fertilization (test tube babies), organ transplantation, organ harvesting, and surrogate parenting. One of the newest opportunities for pastoral counselors is service on hospital-based ethics committees. Medical ethicist Cynthia B. Cohen reflects:

> Ethics committees are developing at a remarkable pace. In 1982, only one percent of American hospitals had established these committees; today, over 60 percent of hospitals with 200 beds or more have them. Nursing homes and dialysis centers are organizing ethics committees as well. A movement that started in a small way is becoming large and significant.[3]

Ethics committees may take several forms. On one hand, they debate the moral and ethical factors inherent in new biomedical issues. On another, they make decisions that will affect the allocation of health care resources, new and limited technologies, and organs available for transplant. Finally, they debate issues involving specific patients, such as the withholding or termination of extraordinary means of medical treatment.

The problem with such committees is an under-representation on the part of Christians who hold the Bible to be an authoritative guide for professional conduct. Hospital-based ethics committees tend to be made up of physicians, nurses and other treatment personnel, attorneys, and an *occasional* pastor. Those pastors who do sit on ethics committees usually have a strong background in Clinical Pastoral Education (CPE), which can have a negative effect on decision-making skills that rely on scriptural guidelines. According to the Pace study,

> all who go through CPE seem to be affected by the characteristic of liberalism that places the locus of authority not in theological or biblical doctrine, but vests it in the example of a religious life. . . . Thus, the CPE training process seems to

3. Cynthia B. Cohen, "Birth of a Network," *Hastings Center Report*, February-March 1988, p. 11.

cause even evangelical and fundamental chaplains to shift their emphasis and trust (at least to some degree) from God's Word and His Spirit to the influence of their presence as persons.[4]

For the average pastor or Christian counselor, however, most counseling opportunities will not take place in the context of an ethics committee but on a one-to-one basis within the ministry of the local church.

## MEDICAL TREATMENT: A KEY COUNSELING ISSUE

Improvements in medical treatment indicate that the incidence of sudden death will continue to lessen. The decrease in fatalities due to heart attacks and stroke, combined with the increase in cancer, results in several factors that will impact the pastoral counseling area.

First, a larger number of people will have an indication of their own deaths. Patients who are informed that they have terminal cancer will have the opportunity to arrange the rest of their lives accordingly, for better or worse. Although there may be a period of physical or mental incapacitation prior to a person's death, the patient will likely call upon the pastor for advice of a spiritual, medical, financial, or family nature while still able to retain a certain amount of control in his or her life.

Because of the increase in the elderly population, the children of patients will be called upon to contribute to the decision-making process with regard to medical care. Here, too, pastors will be consulted not only for spiritual support but also for assistance in making key treatment decisions.

The most common scenario, perhaps, involves the question, "What should I do?" Imagine the possible backdrops in which this question may be asked:

4. Dale K. Pace, *A Chaplains Guide to Effective Jail and Prison Ministries* (Old Tappan, N.J.: Fleming H. Revell, 1973), pp. 100-101. The liberal bias of CPE is explicitly expressed in Jenny Yates Hammett, "A Second Drink at the Well: Theological and Philosophical Content of CPE Origins," *Journal of Pastoral Care* 29 (June 1975): 86-89.

- George, a sixty-eight year old, is informed that he has acute lymphocytic leukemia. Without treatment, he may live six months. With chemotherapy and radiation, his life could be extended by two or three years. George knows, however, that the physical and emotional effects of the treatment are severe. He will lose his hair, become weak, experience nausea and other discomforting physical effects. He goes to his pastor and asks, "What should I do?"
- Mary is seventy-two years old and has been diagnosed with cancer of the esophagus. She was taken to the hospital after she experienced difficulty breathing, and she was placed on a respirator for several days. She is now breathing on her own, though she knows it is inevitable that her breathing will again become impaired and she will once again require the use of a respirator. Her pastor visits her in the hospital where she informs him that she is considering refusing further emergency treatment. She reflects, "I've lived a good life, and I don't want to deal with the discomfort of having to breathe through a machine again. What should I do?"
- Jack is a forty-two-year-old parishioner who informs his pastor that his seventy-year-old father has had a stroke that has left him completely paralyzed. Jack's father can neither speak nor write, and Jack tells his pastor, "I know that Dad wouldn't want to go on living like this. The doctors have told me that, as next-of-kin, I'm his guardian and have the right to have aggressive therapy withheld. What should I do?"
- At the age of fifty-eight Susan has had a myocardial infarction and has gone into cardiac arrest. The paramedics performed CPR and revived her, but two days later she had a massive heart attack and again arrested. The medical staff again performed CPR and revived her, and diagnostic tests have revealed that she is likely to have another coronary attack within days. Knowing she will not be able to live her life as she did prior to hospitalization, she wants her doctor to write a *Do Not Resuscitate* order. She asks her pastor, "What should I do?"

- Bob and Linda are the parents of a teenage daughter who has been in a serious car accident. Their daughter has been in a coma for several weeks, and her physicians concur that it is likely she will remain in a persistent vegetative state. She is being fed by intravenous fluid and a nasogastric tube, and the doctors have recommended terminating her nutrition and hydration. Bob and Linda ask their pastor, "What should we do?"[5]

And so it goes. The old expression that you can't cheat death is no longer as valid as it once was; based on today's technology, many people do seem to cheat death. And as death becomes a process less sudden than it once was, pastors and Christian counselors will be increasingly called upon to help patients and family members reach crucial decisions.

The ultimate criteria in such counseling situations must be Scripture, prayer, and God's will for the patient. Yet it is also important for counselors to be aware of the legal issues involved in the making of life-and-death decisions in the medical environment.

## TREATMENT DECISIONS AND THE COMPETENT PATIENT

The decision of whether to accept treatment options is legally based on the right to self-determination. Competent patients have the ultimate authority in making medical decisions that will affect them. Competence includes two factors: the ability to rationally *decide* whether or not to accept a course of treatment, and the ability to *communicate* that decision to treatment personnel. Communication may be spoken, written, or involve something as abstract as blinking the eyes in direct response to detailed questions by a treatment professional. Likewise, the communication of the patient's own wishes may be made at the time of treatment or in ad-

5. The question of whether nutrition and hydration can be withdrawn from a persistently vegetative patient was addressed by the U.S. Supreme Court in *Cruzan v. Missouri*, 110 S.Ct. 2841 (1990). The Court held that the determination of whether a third party could make such a decision for a patient who had not made his or her wishes known by way of a formal living will was to be left to individual states. It did not address the question of whether the provision or food and water constituted ordinary or extraordinary care.

vance of the patient's becoming too incompetent to rationalize or communicate his or her wishes.

An increasing number of states now recognize the "living will," an instrument by which persons may make their wishes known before the need to make critical decisions arises.[6] Harvard law professor Arthur Miller notes that various states interpret the validity of living wills differently:

> Some of these statutes require that the declaration be made after a person learns of a terminal illness; others allow a healthy person to decide what he would want done should illness or accident render it impossible to make the decision. To prevent a rash decision, one statute requires that at least a two-week period pass between the time when the condition is revealed to the patient and when he signs the will; safeguards include the right to revoke the will orally at any time, and a set period after which it lapses.[7]

The living will is essentially a document that is written by a person while he or she is competent whose provisions are intended to be implemented in the event that the person becomes incompetent or is unable to communicate his or her wishes. A typical living will would read as follows:

> On this ________ day of ________ (month, year), I, __________________, being of sound mind, willfully and voluntarily direct that my dying shall not be artificially prolonged under the circumstances set forth in this declaration:
>
> If at any time I should have an incurable injury, disease, or illness certified to be a terminal condition by two (2) physicians who have personally examined me, one (1) of whom shall be my attending physician, and the physicians have determined that my death is imminent and will occur whether or

6. At this writing, states that recognize the validity of living wills include Alabama, Alaska, Arizona, Arkansas, California, Colorado, Connecticut, Delaware, District of Columbia, Florida, Georgia, Hawaii, Idaho, Illinois, Indiana, Iowa, Kansas, Louisiana, Maine, Maryland, Missouri, Montana, New Hampshire, New Mexico, North Carolina, Oklahoma, Oregon, South Carolina, Tennessee, Texas, Utah, Virginia, Washington, West Virginia, Wisconsin, Wyoming. For a list of relevant statutes, see John K. Veroneau, "In re Gardner: Withdrawing Medical Care from Persistently Vegetative Patients," *Maine Law Review* 41 (1989), pp. 449-50.
7. Arthur Miller, *Miller's Court* (Boston: Houghton Mifflin, 1982), p. 250.

not life-sustaining procedures are utilized and where the application of such procedures would serve only to artificially prolong the dying process, I direct that such procedures be withheld or withdrawn, and that I be permitted to die naturally with only the administration of medication, the administration of food and water, and the performance of any medical procedure that is necessary to provide comfort care or alleviate pain. In the absence of my ability to give directions regarding the use of such life-sustaining procedures, it is my intention that this declaration shall be honored by my family and physician(s) as the final expression of my right to control my medical care and treatment.

I am legally competent to make this declaration, and I understand its full import.[8]

Many ethicists, both Christian and secular, believe that living wills may have a negative impact upon a patient's course of treatment and may also act as a dangerous step toward euthanasia. John Jefferson Davis, professor of systematic theology and ethics at Gordon-Conwell Theological Seminary, writes:

> Drafters of living will legislation have not succeeded in removing the inherent ambiguity in such terms as "terminal illness." Circumstances of terminal illness reflect multitudes of specific factors that are only precisely known in the doctor-patient relationship, and that are very difficult, if not impossible, to specify adequately in the abstractions of legal language. Phrases such as "reasonable hope of recovery," "artificial means," and "extraordinary measures" are in fact quite fluid, given the dynamic nature of medical advances and the complexities of a specific patient's case. Such semantic difficulties, when reflected in the law, are likely to lead to further litigation, rather than giving substantial help in an already difficult area of medicine and morals.
>
> The widespread adoption of living will legislation would also have an unhealthy "chilling" effect on the doctor-patient relationship. Rather than focusing exclusively on the interests

8. Sample Living Will, Maryland Life-Sustaining Procedures Act, reprinted in Beth Spring and Ed Larson, *Euthanasia: Spiritual, Medical & Legal Issues in Terminal Health Care* (Portland: Multnomah, 1988), pp. 207-8.

of the patient, the doctor may fear legal penalties resulting from such legislation and thus be biased toward forms of treatment least likely to provoke a malpractice suit.[9]

Christian medical ethicist Franklin Payne, a physician, argues that living wills lose their effect in light of the fact that the very nature of medicine prevents precise prognoses, and emergency decisions must often be made in a split-second environment:

> The definition of ordinary and extraordinary varies among medical professionals, and medical crises do not allow the needed time for reflection on these proposed desires of the patient nor do they allow for changes in treatment as the patient's condition changes. For example, a patient may arrive at an emergency room with a cardiac arrest. All would agree that every attempt must be used acutely to save this patient's life. Subsequently, the patient may remain in a coma with severe, permanent brain damage after the cause of the cardiac arrest has been treated effectively. The patient may not have desired a respirator, but its use was initially unavoidable. How can a man decide the degree of distress that he is likely to tolerate at some future date?[10]

The bottom line is that medicine is not infallible. While the Bible speaks generally of the sanctity of life, it does not address the many case-specific issues that must be considered in the course of making treatment decisions in this age of technology, nor does Scripture directly address the ambiguity of terms inherent in a living will, such as the difference between routine and extraordinary treatment in a technological age.

We must remain cognizant of the fact that what was extraordinary yesterday may be ordinary today. For example, kidney dialysis was once a rare treatment due to its experi-

9. John Jefferson Davis, *Evangelical Ethics* (Phillipsburg, N.J.: Presbyterian and Reformed, 1985), pp. 184-85.
10. Franklin E. Payne, Jr., *Biblical Medical Ethics: The Christian and the Practice of Medicine* (Milford, Mich.: Mott Media, 1985), p. 200.

mental nature and the availability of dialysis equipment. Today, it is considered a routine, albeit not easy, treatment.

For the pastor or counselor who is called upon to assist a patient or family in making key medical decisions, some guidelines might be appropriate from a legal standpoint.

1. At this writing, there have been no reported lawsuits against pastors who have counseled persons with regard to withholding or terminating treatment. Nonetheless, the counseling offered should be nondirective, and the goal of the counselor should be to help the patient or family make their own decisions. If a counselor specifically says, "I advise you to pull the plug," he or she could be sued by a family member who later questions or regrets such a decision. Even if the suit were unsuccessful, its defense could result in substantial legal expense.
2. The pastor or counselor should recognize his or her own limitations with regard to making recommendations for the implementation, withholding, or termination of treatment. If physicians are not able to discern an accurate prognosis for a patient, surely the counselor will not be able to do so. Therefore, the primary counseling techniques that should be used in such a situation are personal support and prayer.
3. The pastor's or counselor's professional training should include study in medical ethics. This is not currently a part of most seminary or counseling curricula, but as ministry professionals are increasingly called upon to assist in making such decisions, it will be important to demonstrate competency in this area.
4. In conjunction with the above, pastors may wish to consider becoming involved with the ethics committee of a local hospital or nursing facility. As noted earlier, most of the representation on such committees is secular, and it is important for the Christian viewpoint to be represented in the treatment arena.
5. In regard to the making of a living will (or any other type of will), the counselor should not assist the counselee in the

actual drafting of such a document. Since wills are legal documents, this would involve the unauthorized practice of law, and the counselee should be referred to a competent attorney for assistance.

## Other Medical Issues in Counseling

Most of the interaction between medicine, religion, and law centers on cults and fringe religious groups rather than on traditional Christian denominations. Jehovah's Witnesses and Christian Scientists, for example, are known for refusing certain types of medical treatment that would not be objectionable to Christians in general.

One of the most common scenarios in this realm involves the administration of blood transfusion to Jehovah's Witnesses. As in the case of termination-of-treatment issues, the right of self-determination predominates the thinking of most courts, and an adult Jehovah's Witness is permitted to refuse a transfusion even if death is a likely result.

In one recent case, for example, the Florida Supreme Court held that a mother's right to refuse a transfusion was not overridden by the state's interest in maintaining a two-parent home for her minor children.[11] Another case extended this right to a mature minor (then fifteen years old) who refused medical treatment (including blood transfusions) for acute leukemia based on her sincerely held religious beliefs as a Jehovah's Witness.[12]

On the other hand, hospitals will usually petition the courts for an order to override the wishes of parents who refuse to allow transfusions for younger children. Courts generally grant these orders and will also intervene in cases where the patient refusing a transfusion is a pregnant woman whose fetus could be placed in jeopardy.[13]

11. Public Health Trust of Dade County v. Wons, 541 So.2d 96 (S.Ct. Fla. 1989).
12. In re Gregory, 515 N.E.2d 286 (Ill. App. 1987).
13. See Ruth Macklin, "The Inner Workings of an Ethics Committee: Latest Battle over Jehovah's Witnesses," *Hastings Center Report*, February-March 1988, pp. 15-20.

Another controversial area is the issue of refusing medical care in favor of spiritual healing. This primarily affects Christian Scientists, and legal doctrines in this area are in a state of flux at the present time. A number of states that once exempted Christian Scientists and other groups that believe in healing by prayer to the exclusion of medical treatment are revising their laws due to an increase in childhood deaths. In one Oklahoma case, the parents of a three-month-old boy who died of pneumonia were convicted of second-degree manslaughter and sentenced to two years in prison because they did not seek medical attention for the child. Instead, in accordance with the tenets of their religion, the Church of the New Born, they unsuccessfully relied on divine intervention for the boy's healing.[14]

Refusing medical treatment in favor of spiritual healing or prayer is not, by any means, restricted to theological cults or non-Christian sects. The well-known story of Hobart Freeman and the Faith Christian Assembly, in Indiana, is a classic example. While holding to an orthodox Christology (that is, an orthodox definition of the Person, work, and nature of Jesus Christ), Freeman taught that seeing a physician was sinful and indicated a lack of faith on the part of the believer.

Not surprisingly, members of the Faith Assembly had a higher mortality rate than the general population. Although Freeman managed to gather a significant following, he died in 1984 at the age of sixty-four as a result of bronchopneumonia and heart failure, having neither sought nor received any medical treatment for either problem.[15]

Other areas in which Christian counselors may be sought for advice include abortion and substance abuse. The right to abortion is firm at present, though as an absolute right it has recently been given some restrictions by the U.S. Supreme Court.[16] Pastors and Christian counselors who hold

14. Funkhouser v. Oklahoma, 763 P.2d 695 (Okla. Crim. 1988), *cert. denied* 109 S.Ct. 2066 (1989).
15. For a detailed overview of the Faith Assembly, see Bruce Barron, *The Health and Wealth Gospel* (Downers Grove, Ill.: InterVarsity, 1987), pp. 14-34.
16. See, e.g., Webster v. Missouri, 109 S.Ct. 3040 (1989); Hodgson v. Minnesota, 110 S.Ct. 2926 (1990); and Ohio v. Akron Center for Reproductive Health, 110 S.Ct. 2972 (1990).

a pro-life stand need not fear counseling a pregnant woman based on a biblical standard, provided that such counseling does not include physical coercion to prevent an abortion. (For more on this issue, especially in light of Operation Rescue, see chapter 13.)

The only legal difficulty at present in counseling persons regarding substance abuse may occur if a drug abuser brings in his or her drugs and surrenders them to the pastor or counselor. In such a situation, the counselor should turn them over to a legal authority (such as a local police department) as soon as possible. (Not to do so could render the counselor subject to criminal prosecution for the possession of illegal drugs.) Pastors are unconditionally protected by the confidentiality privilege and do not have to reveal the source of the drugs; whether nonpastoral Christian counselors are protected by the confidentiality privilege has not been tested, but prosecution in this instance is highly unlikely.

In the event that an addicted counselee expresses the desire to stop using drugs, he or she should be referred to a medical facility specializing in the treatment of addictions. To directly aid a drug addict in the process of going "cold turkey" is not a criminal offense, but detoxification is a process in which few pastors or counselors are trained and one that requires medical support. If complications develop, the counselor could be sued for negligence because he or she did not refer the counselee to an appropriate facility.

As in other areas, when counseling on medical issues, it is important for pastors and counselors to keep their actions within the scope of spiritual counseling: to refrain from diagnosing, to be nondirective whenever possible, and not to go beyond their level of skills and training.

# 13

# Counseling and Civil Disobedience

Juli Loesch Wiley is the founder and former national coordinator of an organization called Prolifers for Survival, an activist group that stands against both abortion and the nuclear arms race. Wiley exposed some common stereotypes of conservatives and liberals at a workshop several years ago when she commented, "This is my right wing. On my right wing, as we all know, we have what is supposedly the prolife movement: narrow-minded, bigoted, reactionary, Republican Reagan voters. And over here on my left wing, as we all know, we have the dope-smoking, fornicating, hippie unorthodox peace movement."

Wiley continued, "Now, I think we're all big enough to know that this isn't necessarily a true description of political realities. And I think we also know that you can't fly with just a right wing or a left wing; you can only fly if you have two wings and the middle of the bird."[1]

In his seminal study on faith and values in American society, sociologist Robert Wuthnow observes that, as the Christian church moves into the 1990s, we are observing a schism that is geared less toward Christians versus non-Christians than toward conservatives and liberals within Christian denominations.[2]

1. Juli Loesch Wiley, workshop at Pax Christi-USA national conference, Milwaukee, Wisconsin, 16 October 1980.
2. Robert Wuthnow, *The Struggle for America's Soul* (Grand Rapids: Eerdmans, 1989).

In the realm of the law as it affects Christians, the same dichotomy can be observed as we examine the issues of concern to believers (and, for that matter, unbelievers) within the church. Ask a conservative Christian to identify important issues, and the list is a familiar one: freedom to evangelize, school prayer, anti-Christian discrimination, government aid to religious institutions, taxation and the church, and church discipline. Add to these the social issues of abortion and the right to life, public and private morality, the mass media, and a multitude of other social and political issues on which Christians have spoken out over the past decades.

Wuthnow's hypothesis is solid: left is left, right is right, and rarely do they meet. Yet over the past few years, some issues have moved from the liberal to the conservative sphere that have an impact on pastoral and Christian counselors. These include civil disobedience, conscientious objection and the draft, and the sanctuary movement.

A classic illustration documents the impact of the issues we face today. In the early 1960s, liberal and mainline churches were heavily involved in social issues that included the civil rights, early women's rights, and anti-war movements. Conservative Christians tended not to be involved in political issues and, in fact, chided liberals for placing more emphasis on social activism than on the gospel of Jesus Christ.

Beginning with the advent of the Moral Majority, the Christian Roundtable, Concerned Women for America, and other conservative organizations that formed the "New Religious Right" in 1980, the tables have turned. While conservatives still place more emphasis on the biblical gospel than liberals, evangelicals have become involved in social and political issues to the extent that they use many of the same techniques that liberals used in the early 1960s. And liberals have begun to say that conservatives should "stick to the gospel." Paradoxical, to say the least.

## Civil Disobedience: An Overview

Witness, for example, Operation Rescue. When one observes the advent of nonviolent civil disobedience taking place at abortion clinics around the country, there's no doubt that the participants and the issues being addressed are different from the civil disobedience that took place at lunch counters during the early civil rights movement. Yet the techniques are the same.

According to traditional theories of civil disobedience, there are six general conditions that must exist for disobedience to be justified.

1. For a civil law to be broken, it must conflict with a divine law. Civil rights workers perceived that racial discrimination conflicted with the admonition that all persons are created equal, without regard to race or color. The antinuclear movement, much of which is based on religious teachings, perceives that nuclear weapons are sinful and against God's law. Today, Operation Rescue participants perceive that the existence of abortion clinics is against the will of God as revealed in Scripture.
2. There must be a pattern of obedience to the law in the lives of persons committing civil disobedience. Under normal circumstances, when laws are just, persons engaged in nonviolent civil disobedience freely obey the law.
3. There must be no harm to people in an action that includes civil disobedience; the action must be nonviolent in nature. When, for example, Operation Rescue participants act against abortion clinics, they do so by blocking entrances, not by destroying the property.
4. Civil disobedience must be used as a last resort, after all other avenues for correcting an unjust situation have been exhausted.
5. Punishment must be accepted for the action. Essentially, if people commit an act of civil disobedience, they should "pay their dues." An example of this is the refusal of Operation Rescue participants to pay fines for their action, choosing to remain in jail instead. To pay a fine, they reason, would be to admit that their original action was not a necessary one.

6. Finally, the action should be done openly and "in the light" so others will be aware of who committed the action and why.

The general theory of civil disobedience comes not so much from the Bible as from contemporaries such as Gandhi and Martin Luther King, Jr. Lest one assume that civil disobedience in American culture is a liberal phenomenon, however, one need only look back to the Boston Tea Party and other events leading to the nation's founding. Likewise, the Bible contains several examples of civil disobedience, one of the most significant being Jesus' dealing with the moneychangers in the temple (Matthew 21:12-13; Mark 11:15-17; Luke 19:45-46; John 2:13-16).

As I have spoken to both conservative and liberal groups about sociopolitical issues and the use of civil disobedience, two facts have become clear: (1) each faction disagrees with the stand the other has taken on any given issue, but (2) when the actual activities of each faction are examined, they are both found to utilize the same techniques of nonviolent civil disobedience.

Nonetheless, the use of civil disobedience and the advent of Operation Rescue has generated mixed reviews among Christian commentators. Prominent persons opposed to Operation Rescue include Norman Geisler, John MacArthur, and Charles Stanley, while people such as James Dobson, Jerry Falwell, D. James Kennedy, and Pat Robertson support the movement.

## Operation Rescue and the Law

Almost all cases heard thus far dealing with Operation Rescue have been decided against the rescuers. Most cases have been heard on a criminal basis in local courts, but occasionally members of the Operation Rescue movement have attempted to establish the constitutionality of their activities (or the unconstitutionality of their arrests) in the federal court system.

In Philadelphia, on October 5, 1989, a group of rescuers were arrested after they stepped from a public sidewalk onto the property of an abortion clinic during an anti-abortion protest. They brought a civil suit against the city, alleging that their arrests for defiant trespass were unconstitutional and constituted a violation of their free speech rights under the First Amendment. In *Armes v. City of Philadelphia,*[3] the federal district court held that insofar as the property on which they were arrested was private property and that the First Amendment does not create an absolute right of protest, the arrest did not constitute a violation of the First Amendment. This argument has been upheld in several subsequent cases.

Attorneys for the Operation Rescue movement have attempted to offer a "necessity defense" for their clients (another technique borrowed from the peace movement), but thus far the tactic has been unsuccessful. In *Bobo v. Texas,* a state appeals court held that for the necessity defense to be available, (1) there must be some unlawful force being used, and (2) there must be a requirement to the effect that a third person is protected. The court ruled that there was nothing unlawful about the procedures used in a licensed abortion facility, nor anything unlawful about a woman seeking an abortion. Following *Roe v. Wade,*[4] the court also held that the fetus is not a person for the purpose of a third person defense.[5]

In one controversial ruling, a U.S. Court of Appeals held that a group of anti-abortion demonstrators from the Pennsylvania Pro-Life Coalition (not part of Operation Rescue) were liable under the RICO statutes for acts of extortion against an abortion clinic.[6] RICO, or the Racketeer Influenced and Corrupt Organizations Act,[7] provides that any person injured in his or her business or property through racketeering activity can recover the damages he or she sustains threefold.[8] It was designed to work against traditional racketeers and members of organized crime. Although the ruling sent shivers through-

3. Armes v. City of Philadelphia, 706 F.Supp. 1156 (E.D. Pa. 1989).
4. Roe v. Wade, 410 U.S. 113 (1973).
5. Bobo v. Texas, 757 S.W.2d 58 (Tex. App. 1988), *cert. denied,* 109 S.Ct. 2066 (1989).
6. N.E. Women's Center v. McMonagle, 868 F.2d 1342 (3d Cir. 1989), *cert. denied* 110 S.Ct. 261 (1989).
7. Racketeer Influenced and Corrupt Organizations (RICO) Act, 18 U.S.C. 1961-1968.
8. Ibid., sec. 1864.

out the right-to-life movement, it is important to understand that, in the action for which the protesters were convicted, they had on several occasions forcibly entered the plaintiff's abortion clinic, knocked down employees, and damaged equipment. Therefore, the actions did not meet the standards for nonviolent civil disobedience that Operation Rescue stresses in its training.

There are only two ways that the trend toward conviction of Operation Rescue participants will change. One is through a constitutional amendment that reverses *Roe v. Wade*, which is highly unlikely in light of the amendment process (a vote by two-thirds of both houses of Congress, then ratification by two-thirds of the states). The other is a reversal of *Roe v. Wade* by the U.S. Supreme Court, in which case Operation Rescue will have accomplished its goals. This second possibility is viewed as increasingly likely by both sides in the abortion controversy in light of recent decisions by the Court limiting the absolute right to abortion.

At this writing, legislation has been proposed that would make it a federal crime to intentionally prevent an individual from entering a health facility that provides abortion services. Submitted by Senator Alan Cranston (D-Cal.), the *Guarantee of Free Access to Medical Facilities Act*[9] stipulates a potential fine of $250,000, a three-year prison sentence, and restitution for property damage and bodily injury for actions such as those committed by the Operation Rescue movement. While passage of such a bill is unlikely due to the political make-up of Congress as a whole, it is likely that similar bills will be introduced in the future at both the federal and state levels.

## The Role of the Counselor

The theory of civil disobedience becomes relevant to Christian counseling insofar as actions are often coordinated from Christian churches and organizations. Operation Rescue, for example, is not a church-affiliated organization per

9. Guarantee of Free Access to Medical Facilities Act, S. 2321, 101st Cong., 2d Sess. (1990).

se, but it is a distinctly Christian movement.[10] While some pastors are involved with the movement on the front lines, it is also common for them to act as "coordinating" personnel, remaining in the background and providing moral and spiritual support. In theory, this makes them "accessories to the crime." (Although this is not the venue to comprehensively discuss the morality of Operation Rescue, the following observation may be appropriate: While those in the movement deny criminal action based on the priority of following the laws of God versus civil law, the civil law does treat many Operation Rescue activities as criminal in nature.)

Assume, for example, that I gather together a group of Christian bank robbers. We plan the operation, work out logistics, and discuss the getaway. Then I lead my merry band in prayer for the efficient operation of our caper and send them into the world to carry out the plans we have made while I attend to more spiritual matters. I may not have participated in the actual robbery, but the courts will treat me as if I did. I am, in effect, an accessory to the crime.

Nonetheless, there have been no significant cases in which pastors or other persons who have counseled Operation Rescue participants (without participating in civil disobedience actions themselves) have been prosecuted or convicted for their counsel. This could change, since to advocate the commission of a crime (or to counsel a person in a manner that the commission of the crime is determined to be caused by the counseling) might be prosecuted in the future. As we will see in the next chapter, this trend already exists in terms of counseling conscientious objectors and other persons opposed to the draft.

In the meantime, the support of (or opposition to) civil disobedience, whether in terms of Operation Rescue or any other significant social or political issue, may be another area in which the pastor or counselor must prayerfully consider his or her position, regardless of the civil law, in light of the admonition to "obey God rather than men" (Acts 5:29).

10. For more on the background history of the movement, see Randall Terry, *Operation Rescue* (Springdale, Pa.: Whitaker House, 1988).

# 14

# Counseling, Conscientious Objection, and Sanctuary

At the start of a new semester, I often administer a preliminary survey to my students. Asking them to rate the importance of various legal issues impacting the Christian church, I am not surprised to find that the issues rated least important are conscientious objection, the draft, and the sanctuary movement.

There are several reasons for this. Most of my students are conservative and evangelical, and these issues have traditionally been identified with liberal churches. The sanctuary movement is active primarily in mainline denominations, and during times when there is no draft, conscientious objection is perceived to be a moot issue. Yet they are important issues from a legal standpoint and should be examined, albeit briefly, in this volume, since the way the courts deal with them can have a direct impact on Christian counselors.

## Conscientious Objection: An Overview

Conservative Christians tend to identify the issue of conscientious objection with liberal or mainline churches, much as the peace movement is stereotyped as "left wing." Yet there are several evangelical denominations that have a rich tradition that incorporates institutions such as pacifism, conscientious objection, and peace studies. These include the

Mennonites, Old Order Amish, the Church of the Brethren, Brethren in Christ, and the Religious Society of Friends (Quakers).[1] Likewise, there is a significant number of Roman Catholics who, if not total pacifists, are "nuclear pacifists." While holding to the traditional Just War Theory that delineates the conditions necessary to justify their participation in a war, they believe that these conditions cannot be met in an era where the use of nuclear weapons is perceived as a likely possibility.[2]

Likewise, even conservative Christians who do not support conscientious objection from a personal viewpoint see it as a religious rights issue, due as much accommodation as any other sincerely held religious belief. Even those denominations that accept the Just War Theory generally support the individual's right to conscience in the area of conscientious objection.[3]

For the purpose of our treatment here, conscientious objection can be defined as opposition to participating in a war and may be expressed as total opposition, opposition to a particular war (e.g., Vietnam), or opposition to a particular type of military conflict (e.g., nuclear versus conventional, or offensive versus defensive). Under the law, only objection to participating in any or all wars (rather than just to some wars) results in a partial or total exemption from military service, or from conscription into the armed forces of the United

1. I am not attempting to purport here that all members of the groups listed are born-again Christians. The religious doctrine in some of these denominations is geographically unique. On the East Coast, for example, there are large numbers of Quakers who are non-Christian and politically liberal. On the other hand, Mennonites in the East tend to be politically conservative and theologically evangelical, subscribing to traditional biblical doctrines. Moving west of the Mississippi River, however, the trend is reversed: Quakers are the conservative Christians, and Mennonites are liberal.
2. The contemporary application of the Just War Theory, which most nonpacifist Christian churches subscribe to, originated with Augustine in the fourth century. The theory holds, among other things, that a war is justified if it is unjust on one side and just on the other, there's a proportion between the killing done and the good that's accomplished, there's no deliberate killing of the innocent, and the war is declared by a king or political leader.
3. See, for example, Beth Ellen Boyle, ed., *Words of Conscience: Religious Statements on Conscientious Objection*, 10th ed. (Washington, D.C.: National Interreligious Service Board for Conscientious Objectors, 1983).

States.[4] Those who are granted such an exemption are, however, required to perform two years of noncombatant or nonmilitary alternative service.[5]

Though most evangelicals are politically conservative on the issues of war and peace, the necessity of being prepared to counsel a potential conscientious objector is established by the interaction that often takes place between pacifist and nonpacifist denominations.[6] Biblical Theological Seminary in Pennsylvania, for example, where I have taught law courses to theology students, pastors, counselors, and attorneys, is in the middle of a geographic area with a large Mennonite population. The largest Christian high school in the area is Mennonite, and many students who attend the school come from conservative Baptist, Presbyterian, and other evangelical churches. Even if the students do not study peace issues in the context of their home or church life, they are introduced to the doctrines of pacifism and nonviolent resistance at school, after which they approach their own pastors or others at their church for counseling on these issues.

4. Traditionally, the courts have upheld total opposition to war as legitimate. Selective objectors, or those who are not opposed to war *in toto*, have not been recognized as conscientious objectors under the law. (See, e.g., Gillette v. United States, 407 U.S. 437 [1971].) The closest the Supreme Court has come to allowing selective objection was in a 1955 case involving a Jehovah's Witness who had been denied exemption because he had expressed willingness to fight in a "theocratic war" on the orders of Jehovah and justified the use of force to defend "his ministry, Kingdom interest, and his fellow brethren." The Court, in reversing his conviction, expressed doubt that the Witnesses actually contemplated a theocratic war, as well as doubt that "the yardstick of Congress includes within its measure such spiritual wars between the powers of good and evil where the Jehovah's Witnesses, if they participate, will do so without carnal weapons" (Sicurella v. United States, 345 U.S. 385, 391 [1955]).
5. There are essentially two types of conscientious objectors: those who are opposed only to participating in combat, and those opposed to performing any type of service in the military. Conscientious objectors opposed to combatant service are still subject to the draft but are assigned to noncombat roles (e.g., medical corps, administrative positions). Those opposed to military service *in toto* are required to perform two years of alternative service in a civilian capacity (e.g., working in a hospital). The second type of objector is the most common.
6. For examples of the biblical basis for military conscription, see Numbers 1:2-3; 26:2; and 31:3-7. For biblical statements on exemption from military service, see Numbers 1:49 and Deuteronomy 20:5-8.

Within thirty days of their eighteenth birthday, young men are required to register for the draft.[7] In an environment where young people are exposed to peace studies or pacifist doctrine, questions are raised in such a manner that confusion often results as they reach the age where they are to fulfill their registration responsibility. Therefore, pastors and counselors, even in conservative denominations, must be prepared to deal with the issues of draft registration and conscientious objection.

## CONSCIENTIOUS OBJECTION AS A RELIGIOUS RIGHT

Historically, the right to conscientious objection dates back to colonial times. According to attorney John P. C. Fogarty, "The moral and religious scruples of objectors to participation in war have long been respected in the United States, extending into early colonial times; legal protection for religious objectors was provided as early as 1673 in Rhode Island."[8] The Continental Congress also acknowledged the position of conscientious objectors when they passed a resolution in 1775:

> As there are some people who, from religious principles, cannot bear arms in any case, this Congress intend no violence to their consciences, but earnestly recommend it to them, to contribute liberally in this time of universal calamity, to the relief of their distressed brethren in the several colonies, and do all other services to their oppressed Country, which they can consistently with their religious principles.[9]

7. Registration for the draft affects male American citizens only; young women are exempt from the registration. When draft registration was implemented in 1980, several persons challenged the exclusion of women from the registration requirement. A three-judge federal district court panel held that the exclusion violated the Equal Protection and Due Process clauses in the Fifth and Fourteenth Amendments to the U.S. Constitution and declared the Military Selective Service Act unconstitutional. The U.S. Supreme Court reversed, holding that Congress acted within its constitutional authority when it authorized the registration of men, and not women, under the Act (Rostker v. Goldberg, 453 U.S. 57 [1981]).
8. John P. C. Fogarty, "The Right Not to Kill: A Critical Analysis of Conscientious Objection and the Problem of Registration," *New England Law Review* 18 (1985): 657.
9. *Journals of the Continental Congress, 1774-1789, May 10–September 20,* ed. Worthington C. Ford (34 vols.), 2:1775 (Washington, D.C.: Government Printing Office, 1904-1937), p. 139.

In modern times, with the establishment of the Selective Service, the *Selective Draft Act of 1917* also contained a provision for conscientious objectors:

> Nothing in this Act contained shall be construed to require or compel any person to serve in any of the forces herein provided for who is found to be a member of any well-recognized religious sect or organization at present organized and existing and whose existing creed or principles forbid its members to participate in war in any form.[10]

The 1917 act expired after World War I, and there was no draft until 1940, when the Universal Military Training Act took effect. Despite the early acts, however, it was common during the first two world wars for pacifist conscientious objectors to be sentenced to prison for their beliefs.

The acts traditionally granted exemption to members of the historical peace churches (Brethren, Mennonite, and Quaker), but the exemptions were expanded in 1948 to include other persons who believed in a Supreme Being. Later revisions removed even the requirement of belief in a Supreme Being but were still based on religious principles:

> Nothing contained in this title [section 451s to 471a of this appendix] shall be construed to require any person to be subject to combatant training and service in the armed forces of the United States who, by reason of religious training and belief, is conscientiously opposed to participation in war in any form. As used in this subsection, the term "religious training and belief" does not include essentially political, sociological, or philosophical views, or a merely personal moral code.[11]

Despite the religious restriction imposed by Congress, however, the courts have allowed exemptions for nonreligious reasons by broadening the definition of religion to include deeply held religious, moral, or ethical philosophy. According to Gail White Sweeney, "Looking at the C.O. ex-

10. Selective Draft Act, ch. 15, sec. 4, 40 Stat. 76, 78 (1917).
11. 50 U.S.C. 456(j) (1976).

emption from the Civil War through the Vietnam War, one notes that the general tendency has been to broaden the exemption. This liberalizing has been done both by congressional act and (when Congress has been uncooperative) by administrative and judicial interpretation."[12]

Though the courts have broadened the right to conscientious objection, the right itself is legislative in nature. To those who have declared their belief that conscientious objection is a constitutional right, the Supreme Court has replied that

> there is no such principle in the Constitution, fixed or otherwise. The conscientious objector is relieved from the obligation to bear arms in obedience to no constitutional provision, express or implied, but because, and only because it has accorded with the policy of Congress to relieve him. . . . The privilege of the native-born conscientious objector to avoid bearing arms comes not from the Constitution, but from the acts of Congress. That body may grant or withhold the exemption as in its wisdom it sees fit; and if it be withheld, the native-born conscientious objector cannot successfully assert the privilege.[13]

Functionally, conscientious objection today involves the legislative accommodation of a person's religious opposition to participation in war of any type, though religious opposition does not necessarily connote belief in a Supreme Being nor any other doctrine that is theistically grounded. Statistically, however, most religious objectors are members of Christian churches that hold beliefs that include what they perceive to be a biblical concept of pacifism.

## Counseling the Conscientious Objector

In the draft registration that took place during the Vietnam War era and earlier periods, young men had the opportu-

12. Gail White Sweeney, "Conscientious Objection and the First Amendment," *Akron Law Review* 14 (1980): 73-74.
13. United States v. Macintosh, 283 U.S. 605, 623-24 (1931), rev'd. on other grounds by Girouard v. United States, 328 U.S. 61 (1946).

nity to declare their conscientious objection when registering for the draft at the age of eighteen. However, in the current draft registration, signed into law by President Jimmy Carter in 1980, they do not have the opportunity to make their conscientious objection known in a manner that the Selective Service will acknowledge:

> Someone who registers for the draft and plans to file for a deferment will not be allowed to claim a deferment until after Selective Service sends them an induction order. This means that once they register and receive their "verification notice" the only other direct response they will receive from Selective Service is an induction order. Selective Service will keep no record of deferment claims made before an induction order.[14]

The person who has taken the time to consider the nature of conscription and conscientious objection generally knows where he or she stands on these issues. Most young people, especially those who are not members of a traditional peace church, have not considered them at all. Therefore, in the event of a draft, it is unlikely that most young people will have been able to determine their position in the short period of time from receipt of an induction order until their reporting date. According to Jon Landau, former general counsel for the Central Committee for Conscientious Objectors,

> Selective Service has made it very clear that they intend to process various kinds of claims at the very last minute. That makes this registration a much more critical time for young people to consider what their position is. There simply won't be enough time for people to make up their minds as to what they'll do with respect to the draft. We know from our draft counseling experiences back during the Vietnam years that young people will not be able to make up their minds on these complex issues in that ten-day period [from induction to reporting]. If they wait until then, most of them will just be

14. Bill Galvin and Larry Spears, "Selective Service Proposes New Regulations," *CCCO News Notes*, Winter 1981, p. 1.

pushed into the draft. They'll be in the military before they even have a chance to think things over.[15]

The most important goal for the counselor, then, is to ensure that a young person know where he or she stands in relation to military service, the draft, and his willingness to participate in a military conflict. However, draft counseling should, by nature, be nondirective for a number of reasons.

First, dealing with conscientious objection is one of the few areas in which the counselor is actually dealing with legal issues per se in the course of counseling. Thus, the counseling should be limited to explaining a young person's legal responsibilities and options for exemption and helping him determine his own position. In April 1969 the American Bar Association Committee on Unauthorized Practice of Law stated that, insofar as draft counseling is restricted to advising registrants about their status and procedures under the Selective Service System before a draft board or appeal board (which does not include representing him in a court of law), there is no violation of statutes prohibiting the unauthorized practice of law. According to the Central Committee for Conscientious Objectors,

> the Committee found that Congress, in passing the draft law, designed a system that meant to exclude attorneys from the administrative process and planned a system to be administered informally by laymen. Since this was the intent of Congress, a state would violate the supremacy clause (U.S. Constitution, Article VI, Section 2) if it tried to interfere with the federal scheme and prosecute the lay draft counselor.[16]

Another reason draft counseling should be nondirective is that, if the counselor is sympathetic to the conscientious objector and advocates the breaking of the law, he or she could be convicted of violating the Military Selective Service Act, which provides that any person who knowingly coun-

15. John Landau, interview by the author, 4 January 1981.
16. "The Counselor and the Law," *CCCO Military Counselor's Manual* (update of 1 April 1974), pp. A3-6.

sels, aids, or abets another person to refuse or evade registration or service in the armed forces may be punished by imprisonment for up to five years, a fine of up to $250,000, or both.[17] Therefore, counselors who are members of traditional peace churches must be careful in expressing their own opinions in a direct counseling situation insofar as their words could be construed as specific advice to the counselee that he shouldn't cooperate with the government.

This is a common occurrence in dealing with the issue of nonregistration. Some young people in peace churches, for example, believe that, if it is immoral to participate in war, then it is also immoral to register for such participation. Therefore, they have refused to even register with the Selective Service at their eighteenth birthday. For those counselors who are sympathetic with them, it is important to understand that advising counselees not to register can result in criminal prosecution for the counselor as well.[18]

In 1980, when the draft registration was resumed, the peace movement took the alarmist stance that "every time there's been a draft registration, there's been a draft; and every time there's been a draft, there's been a war." Yet after eight years of the Reagan administration, one of the most

17. 50 U.S.C. 462(a). This section deals with a one-on-one or formal counseling situation. Advocating resistance in a public (nondirect counseling) context does not violate this provision of the Act. (The reader should take note that I am not advocating a particular stand on the part of the counselor. For the curious, however, I am neither a pacifist nor do I belong to a traditional peace church, though as an expression of religious freedom I respect persons who hold such a position.)
18. Early in the current draft registration, the government adopted a selective enforcement policy, prosecuting only those young men who refused to register in a public manner. In one case that went before the U.S. Supreme Court, David Wayte, a political resister from Pasadena, California, argued that he was being selectively punished for his expression of ideas in violation of the First and Fifth Amendments. Writing for the Court, Justice Lewis Powell noted that the country has a compelling interest in ensuring its safety, and defended the selective enforcement policy, since it "placed no more limitation on speech than was necessary to ensure registration for the national defense" (Wayte v. United States, 105 S.Ct. 1524, 1533 [1985]).

    At present, the government has dropped the selective enforcement policy in favor of an "active compliance" policy. Rather than prosecuting nonregistrants, a series of Congressional statutes has resulted in nonregistrants losing their eligibility for federal financial assistance in higher education. While nonregistrants will be prosecuted for fraud if they seek federal aid under false pretenses, the government is not currently prosecuting persons for nonregistration per se.

conservative political administrations in the nation's history, the peace was maintained.

There is currently no military draft, and, absent conscription, the issue of counseling conscientious objectors is not of critical importance. Nonetheless, it is inevitable that at some point, there will again be a draft, and counselors should be prepared to deal with the issue.[19] At this writing, for example, Senator Mark Hatfield recently introduced a bill to discontinue the draft registration.[20] Less than two months after the bill's introduction, however, Iraq invaded Kuwait and thousands of American troops were sent to the Middle East on alert status.

One item that is of current relevance is the fact that advising a young person to break the law through noncooperation with draft registration requirements renders the counselor liable to criminal prosecution. As noted in the last chapter, this is not the case with pastors or counselors who support or advise persons participating in the Operation Rescue movement. However, the draft precedent could be used as a justification to prosecute counselors who advocate illegal activities in an Operation Rescue action and should be watched closely in future cases.

## Sanctuary: A Movement for the Nineties

One other trend that has its roots in liberal and mainline churches and that has been negatively dealt with in legal cases that could have detrimental effects on evangelical

19. The information in this chapter is hardly intended to prepare a pastor or Christian counselor to do draft counseling. For the counselor seeking more information in this area, there are three organizations that specialize in counseling conscientious objectors and training others to do so: the Central Committee for Conscientious Objectors in Philadelphia, Pa., a secular organization; the Mennonite Central Committee in Akron, Pa., the social service arm of the Mennonite and Brethren in Christ churches; and the National Interreligious Service Board for Conscientious Objectors (NISBCO) in Washington, D.C. All three groups are also prepared to provide counseling support for conscientious objectors who are already serving in the armed forces. All three have published counselors' manuals and other resources; the most current draft counseling manual (and the most well written) is by Charles A. Maresca, Jr., ed. (*NISBCO Draft Counselor's Manual*, 5th ed. [Washington, D.C.: National Interreligious Service Board for Conscientious Objectors, 1989]).
20. The Selective Service Standy Act, S. 2681, introduced May 24, 1990.

Christians is the contemporary sanctuary movement. Members of the sanctuary movement are engaged in smuggling Central American refugees into the United States and harboring them from what they perceive to be oppressive governments and regimes in countries such as El Salvador, Guatamala, and Nicaragua. Historically, the movement is grounded in the tradition of the Underground Railroad of the nineteenth century, as well as based in the doctrines of liberation theology prevalant in both Catholic and Protestant churches in Central America.

In the United States, denominations that have expressed support for (or have participated in) the sanctuary movement include the American Baptist Churches in the U.S.A., Evangelical Lutheran Church in America, the Presbyterian Church (U.S.A.), and the Religious Society of Friends (Quakers). Based on its identification with liberation theology, conservative evangelicals tend to be against the sanctuary movement.

In one recent sanctuary case, the U.S. Court of Appeals for the Ninth Circuit held that the convictions of sanctuary movement participants who violated immigration law after they had smuggled, transported, and harbored illegal aliens into the United States were not prevented by the Free Exercise clause of the First Amendment.[21] Among other conclusions, the court rejected the defendants' use of the necessity defense and their allegations of selective prosecution.

In a related case that could have significant impact on evangelical pastors and Christian counselors, the same court commented on the infiltration of churches by agents from the United States Immigration and Naturalization Service:

> From approximately March 1984 to January 1985, several INS agents wearing "body bugs" infiltrated four Arizona churches. The investigations were conducted without search warrants and without probable cause to believe that the surveillance of the churches would uncover evidence of criminal activity. The agents attended and surreptitiously tape recorded several services including an ecumenical worship service offered by the

21. United States v. Aguilar, 871 F.2d 1436 (9th Cir. 1989), *superseded* 883 F.2d 662 (9th Cir. 1989).

Camelback and Sunrise Presbyterian Churches in Phoenix, regular Sunday morning worship services at Southside Presbyterian Church in Tuscon, and Bible study classes at Alzona Lutheran Church in Phoenix. During the surveillance the agents recorded prayers, hymns, and Bible readings.[22]

In ruling that the churches had standing to sue the government, the court cited the chilling effect of the government's surveillance as reported by the plaintiffs:

> Members have withdrawn from active participation in the churches, a Bible study group has been canceled for lack of participation, clergy time has been diverted from regular pastoral duties, support for the churches has declined, and congregants have become reluctant to seek pastoral counseling and are less open in prayers and confessions. . . .
>
> When congregants are chilled from participating in worship activities, when they refuse to attend church services because they fear the government is spying on them and taping their every utterance, all as alleged in the complaint, we think a church suffers organizational injury because its ability to carry out its ministries has been impaired.[23]

Keeping in mind that the law treats all religions equally, it is important to note that, whether or not one supports the goals or activities of the sanctuary movement, the government's treatment of the movement could just as easily be directed at conservative churches involved in other social or political issues. Therefore, in the same way agents might tape services at a sanctuary church, the infiltration of evangelical

22. The Presbyterian Church (U.S.A.) v. United States, 870 F.2d 518, 520 (9th Cir. 1989).
23. Ibid. at 521-22. In December 1990, a U.S. District Court in Arizona held on remand (after a further hearing in the lower court) that the government violated the First Amendment rights of church groups when it infiltrated and secretly tape-recorded the religious gatherings. The court rejected the churches' contention that their Fourth Amendment rights against unreasonable search and seizure were violated but held that the government "is constitutionally precluded from unbridled and inappropriate covert activity which has as its purpose or objective the abridgment of the First Amendment freedoms of those involved" (The Presbyterian Church [U.S.A.] v. United States, No. CIV-86-0072 [D. Ariz. 1990]). It is highly likely that the case is not settled and that future appeals will be filed.

services or of planning sessions for Operation Rescue actions is not inconceivable. This will only result in the same chilling effect upon church attendance, program participation, and the Christian counseling ministry.

As noted in the early pages of this book, just because a person is paranoid doesn't mean there's not a reason to be. Regardless of the dichotomy between conservative and liberal thinking, the sanctuary issue is an illustration of the need to ensure that the free exercise of religion doesn't become vulnerable to inappropriate entanglement from any quarters.

# 15

## Counseling and the Cults

The scene: you are approached by Tom and Joan Roberts, whose son Fred is a nineteen-year-old college student. They inform you that Fred has recently joined the Church of Divine Devotion, that he has become increasingly distant and moody with them, and that they fear for his safety.

Our scenario is not an unusual one; it has been repeated countless times since the "age of the cults" took hold in the late 1960s. Tom and Joan don't know much about the Church of Divine Devotion, but based on the change in Fred's attitude they're sure it's a cult. They believe that Fred has been coerced into becoming a member of the group, and they are considering hiring a deprogrammer in an attempt to win back their son.

Yet this scene is almost stereotypical in nature, for many more people become involved with cults than college students away from home for the first time. Sometimes the roles are reversed, with children expressing fears that their parents have become involved with a cult. To understand the legal ramifications of dealing with such a situation in counseling, it is important to have a solid understanding of what connotes a "cult."

### The Many Definitions of a Cult

Having been a student of the theology of cults and sects for a number of years, I have become convinced that although this has become a popular field of study for Christians, our treatment of cults tends to exhibit a sense of "tunnel vision." Within Christian theology, cults are usually defined based on their Christology, or identification of the Person, work, and nature of Jesus Christ. Those groups that hold a scriptural view of the identity of Jesus are Christian, those that do not are cults. An example of this comes from the late Walter Martin, who defined a cult as "a group of people polarized around someone's interpretation of the Bible" and "characterized by major deviations from orthodox Christianity relative to the cardinal doctrines of the Christian faith, particularly the fact that God became man in Jesus Christ."[1]

Yet cults may also be defined from the sociological and psychological perspectives. Ronald Enroth notes that there are at least three basic approaches to defining cults: sensational (or popular), sociological, and theological:

> A sensational approach to cults is built on journalistic accounts in the popular press which frequently focus on the dramatic and sometimes bizarre aspects of cultic behavior. A sociological definition includes the authoritarian, manipulative, totalistic and sometimes communal features of cults. A theological definition involves some standard of orthodoxy.[2]

Basing her work on Enroth's earlier research, Ruth Tucker of the Trinity Evangelical Divinity School notes that while many cults could fit into more than one category, most of them can be classified under any of six primary categories:

- *Eastern mystical* (Krishna Consciousness, Transcendental Meditation, Divine Light Mission, and the Rajneesh Ashram)
- *Aberrational Christian* (Children of God, The Way International, Church of the Living Word)
- *Psychospiritual or self-improvement* (Scientology, est, Silva Mind Control, Synanon)

1. Walter Martin, *The Rise of the Cults* (Santa Ana, Calif.: Vision House, 1980), p. 12.
2. Ronald Enroth, *A Guide to Cults and New Religions* (Downers Grove, Ill.: InterVarsity, 1983), p. 12.

- *Electic-Syncretistic* (The Unification Church, the Baha'i Movement)
- *Psychic-occult-astral* (The New Age Movement, Church Universal and Triumphant, Eckankar, Association for Research and Enlightenment)
- *Institutionalized or established* (Mormons, Jehovah's Witnesses, Christian Scientists)[3]

Psychology tends to define cults as groups that practice "coercive persuasion" or brainwashing techniques.[4] Combining a theological and psychological perspective, Bob Larson cites the things that many cults share in common: (1) a centralized authority that tightly structures both philosophy and lifestyle; (2) a "we" versus "they" complex, pitting the supposed superior insights of the group against a hostile, outside culture; (3) a commitment for each member to proselytize intensively the unconverted; and (4) an entrenched isolationism that divorces the devotee from the realities of the world at large.[5]

The problem with any definition is that the standard for classifying a cult is open-ended; it often boils down to any group that you or I disagree with, whether in terms of theology, behavior, or recruiting techniques. To the non-Christian for example, cultists may include evangelicals, fundamentalists, Pentecostals, and charismatics. Sociologist Stuart A. Wright observes:

> The term "cult" has been applied indiscriminately to such groups as Catholic Charismatics, Jews for Jesus, Maranatha Campus Ministries, and the Moral Majority. Jews for Jesus, a Hebrew-Christian missionary organization, has been the object of growing anti-cult activity among some traditional Jewish leaders and organizations, despite the lack of empirical evidence for brainwashing. Ted Patrick, the "father" of deprogramming, has asserted that "Falwell has more persons under

3. Ruth A. Tucker, *Another Gospel: Alternative Religions and the New Age Movement* (Grand Rapids: Academie Books, 1989), p. 21.
4. See, e.g., Thomas and Jacqueline Keiser, *The Anatomy of Illusion* (Springfield, Ill.: Charles C. Thomas, 1987).
5. Bob Larson, *Larson's Book of Cults*, rev. ed. (Wheaton, Ill.: Tyndale, 1989), p. 14.

'mind control' than Reverend Moon" and that "Falwell leads the biggest cult in the nation." One recent "cult" targeted by deprogrammers appears to be the Assemblies of God denomination.[6]

In a recent book titled *Cults: Faith, Healing, and Coercion*, Mark Galanter, a professor of psychiatry at the New York University School of Medicine, describes a "typical" Catholic charismatic meeting:

> Neophytes would report their experiences of religious revival, often revealing that this had followed their involvement in the drug subculture. States of altered consciousness were called "gifts of the Holy Spirit" and were expected to lead members to a spiritual rebirth. These experiences included glossolalia, involuntary motor activity, and trances, all generated by the dynamics of the prayer meeting.[7]

The extent to which any group could be considered a cult is illustrated by Ted Patrick, referred to above as the "father" of deprogramming. Patrick has gone so far as to state, "The Bible will drive you crazy if you take it literally. . . . It's one of the biggest rackets the world has ever known, this religious bit."[8]

From the counseling perspective, the interaction between cults and the law will generally center on groups that use coercive techniques to recruit or convert new members. These techniques include diet manipulation, sleep deprivation, group pressure and "love bombing," isolation and separation, or other techniques that result in cognitive restructuring and personality alteration.

Fact: as a counselor, you will perceive a different approach from a person, depending upon the nature of the group his or her family member has joined. For example, whereas the issue of coercive persuasion arises if someone joins the

6. Stuart A. Wright, *Leaving Cults: The Dynamics of Defection* (Washington, D.C.: Society for the Scientific Study of Religion, 1987), p. 2.
7. Mark Galanter, *Cults: Faith, Healing, and Coercion* (New York: Oxford University Press, 1989), p. 79.
8. Ted Patrick, interview by Jim Siegleman et al., *Playboy*, March 1979, pp. 68, 83.

Unification Church, Krishna Consciousness movement, Church Universal and Triumphant, or Rajneesh Ashram, rarely is a concern for a person's intrinsic physical safety expressed if he or she becomes a Mormon or Jehovah's Witness.

Biblically, of course, there's no difference between a cult that allegedly practices "mind control" techniques and one that doesn't: "And the witness is this, that God has given us eternal life, and this life is in His Son. He who has the Son has the life; he who does not have the Son of God does not have the life" (1 John 5:11-12). Psychologically, however, there's a world of difference. It's one thing to be deceived by a false theological argument per se but quite another to join a cult as the result of coercive recruiting techniques.

What is important from the counselor's perspective, in part, is how the cults are viewed under the law. The answer, for better or worse, is that they are viewed in the same manner as any other religious sect, including Christianity.

## CULTS AND THE LAW

As discussed in chapter 3, the law does not restrict a person's right to believe anything he or she chooses, although there may be restrictions upon action based on a religious belief. This principle is not limited to cults but has also been held valid when applied to "fringe groups" within Christianity. In *Bunn v. North Carolina*, for example, the U.S. Supreme Court upheld the constitutionality of an ordinance against snake handling by rural churches that profess to be Christian and believe in a literal interpretation of Mark 16:18.[9]

We do know two facts that set the stage for how the law deals with cults. First, applying the principles of *Reynolds v.*

9. Bunn v. North Carolina, 336 U.S. 942 (1949). This is perhaps the most well-known case centering on the handling of snakes or drinking of strychnine, fairly common practices among rural white people in pockets of the South, who base their activities on Jesus' statement in Mark 16:18. The state court of North Carolina held that the safety of the public outweighed the free exercise clause of the First Amendment and sustained an ordinance prohibiting snake handling. (The consideration of whether or not such groups are Christian or cultic I'll leave for the reader to decide. Not having a comprehensive picture of their theology, I must reserve judgment, though snake handling and the drinking of poison certainly don't impress me as valid activities for Christian churches.)

*United States* in reverse, while *action* based on religious belief may be regulated (e.g., polygamy), the *belief* itself may not be regulated.[10] Quoting Thomas Jefferson's well-known 1802 letter to the Danbury Baptist Association, the Court noted, "The legislative powers of the government reach actions only, and not opinions."[11] Second, while the courts may inquire as to the sincerity of a person's beliefs, neither judicial nor legislative inquiry may be made into the truth or falsehood of those beliefs.[12]

The result is that, legally, the cults are to be treated no differently than the Christian church. This, of course, results in the proverbial good-news bad-news situation. The bad news is that it is difficult to regulate the recruiting techniques of cults; the good news is that any restrictions upon the cults would, by nature, also impact Christians, and the church enjoys the same legal freedom to evangelize as does any other group.

Witness, for example, the protests following the release of the Martin Scorcese's 1988 film *The Last Temptation of Christ.* Christians, exhibiting righteous indignation that was not unjustified, began lobbying for the passage of an anti-blasphemy law to prevent future similar treatments of the gospel.

The problem, however, is that the law cuts both ways. If such a law were passed (which is highly unlikely), the right of Christians openly to declare other religious beliefs to be false would also be impinged.

The result, then, is that we have an open marketplace that ensures the free exchange of ideas. Even wrong ideas. For better or worse, this includes recruiting techniques that are deceptive in nature. According to Thomas and Jacqueline Keiser, "Deception in recruiting and other subtle forms of destructive persuasion are not by themselves illegal."[13] All too often, even Christian churches tend to "accentuate the posi-

10. Reynolds v. United States, 98 U.S. 145 (1878).
11. Ibid. at 164.
12. United States v. Ballard, 322 U.S. 78 (1944). For background on the *Ballard* case, see chapter 3, note 4.
13. Keiser, p. 66.

tive and eliminate the negative" through the presentation, for example, of a "name it and claim it" approach to the gospel.

The law assumes that the decision to join a religious group, whether Christian or cultic, is made based on a person's free choice. Yet the coercive methods often exhibited by cults raise questions as to the legal options that exist in dealing with a situation in which someone has joined a group that practices such techniques.

## Deprogramming and the Law

Ted Patrick developed his techniques of coercive or involuntary deprogramming in the early 1970s. The problem was that, in an attempt to break a person's loyalty to a cultic group, Patrick, who did not operate from a Christian worldview, used many of the same coercive techniques that the cults had been using.

In coercive deprogramming, a cult member, at the request of a parent or concerned relative, is physically abducted from the cult and taken to a hidden location (often a motel room or the home of a relative). The cult member is confronted with facts about the cult that he or she was not exposed to while in the confines of the cult's environment.

If the deprogramming is successful, the matter ends. The person leaves the cult, and there is no legal repercussion. On the other hand, if unsuccessful, both the deprogrammers and the persons who contracted for their services can face both civil and criminal charges, including kidnapping, false imprisonment, assault and battery, outrageous conduct, and intentional infliction of emotional distress. The cults not only encourage such actions but often pay the legal costs involved.

There have, however, been cases in which the courts have absolved parents of civil and criminal charges for deprogramming. One of the most notable is *Peterson v. Sorlien,*[14] in which the parents of a young woman who was a member of The Way International forcibly detained her at the home of a family friend. For the first three days of a sixteen-day period

14. Peterson v. Sorlien, 299 N.W.2d 123 (S.Ct. Minn. 1980).

she resisted the efforts of deprogrammers hired by her parents, but then she began to come around and renounce the group. Shortly thereafter, she reinitiated contact with her boyfriend, also a member of The Way, with the object of convincing him to leave the group as well. However, she subsequently rejoined the group and sued her parents and the deprogrammers for unlawful imprisonment and emotional distress.

In a jury trial, the charges of unlawful imprisonment against her parents were dismissed, but the jury awarded nominal and punitive damages against the deprogrammers. The verdict was upheld by the Minnesota Supreme Court. However, the court's ruling in *Peterson* was based on the fact that, after the first three days, Peterson had remained with her parents voluntarily.

At one time, courts granted conservatorships that allowed young people involved in coercive cults to be removed and deprogrammed legally. However, there has been a sharp decrease in this trend due to a wider interpretation of the Free Exercise clause on the part of the courts. In *Katz v. Superior Court,*[15] for example, a California appeals court held that "without demonstrable evidence of grave impairment, a conservatorship statute cannot be used to deprive a believer of his freedom of action by means of an involuntary treatment like deprogramming."[16]

The main problem with deprogramming, however, is that the same techniques that are used against cultists can be used against Christians. Legal scholar John Eidsmoe reflects:

> I believe forcible deprogramming is dangerous. While I have the greatest sympathy for parents whose children are involved in cults, I am convinced the dangers of deprogramming outweigh any possible advantages.
>
> First, adult cult members are citizens with constitutional rights. The First Amendment protects their right to choose their own religion. That right must be reserved inviolate.

15. Katz v. Superior Court, 73 Cal. App. 3d 952, 988-89 (1977).
16. Kaiser, p. 95.

Second, deprogramming is a threat to Christians. The law makes no distinctions between traditional Christian denominations and the cults. If deprogramming can be used against cultists, why not against Christians as well?

As we have seen, many mental health professionals regard all religion as a pathological symptom of mental illness. To many such persons, evangelical Christianity is just another cult.[17]

## Implications for the Counselor

The enigma of the cults is compounded by the fact that many groups have a degree of acceptance today that they did not enjoy a decade ago, when the memories of Jim Jones and the mass suicides by members of The People's Temple at Jonestown were still fresh. Witness, for example, the respectability of the *Washington Times*, a newspaper affiliated with the Unification Church yet lauded by many evangelical Christians because of its conservative coverage of political issues. (After all, does anyone traveling through Utah refuse to stay at motels in that state, where most rooms have the Book of Mormon rather than a Gideon Bible?) Sadly, it seems, time breeds not only accommodation, but acceptance. These are the days when Krishna devotees no longer have shaved heads with a telltale tuft of hair at the back, when students of Silva Mind Control and Transcendental Meditation hold executive positions in major corporations, and when members of the Unification Church are integrated into society as a whole rather than selling roses on street corners.

It is important for the pastor or counselor to remain cognizant of the fact that when counseling a parent (or another family member) of a cultist, that person is the counselee, not the cultist. Direct intervention with the cultist is precluded simply by the fact that he or she is not in your office.

When the victim of a coercive cult is a minor, a court order may be obtained to rescue the child from the cult. This, however, is a matter for an attorney to handle, and you

17. John Eidsmoe, *The Christian Legal Advisor*, rev. ed. (Grand Rapids: Baker, 1987), p. 333.

should be careful not to counsel a parent in such a manner that you appear to be offering legal advice. The best course of action, in this case, is to refer the parent to a lawyer.

Likewise, in cases of divorce in which the custodial parent places his or her child in a cultic environment, the noncustodial parent may be able to seek court action *if* he or she can prove that the child is in a destructive environment. Based on constitutional principles, however, this will be dependent upon neutral factors involving the treatment of the child, not upon religious or doctrinal teachings (which, by nature, the court cannot consider).

In *LeDoux v. LeDoux,*[18] for example, the Nebraska Supreme Court affirmed a lower court holding that the rights of a noncustodial parent may be monitored when that parent's religion differs from that of the custodial parent. In this case, the court held that the child of a Catholic mother was suffering from severe stress due to the religious practices of his father, a Jehovah's Witness. The religion of his mother, the custodial parent, took precedence over that of the noncustodial parent. Note, however, that the decision was based on psychological rather than doctrinal factors and, had the child's father been the custodial parent, the situation could have been reversed. The law does, indeed, cut both ways.

From the standpoint of apologetics, the gospel of Jesus Christ is well able to stand up to attack by the cults. Therefore, when a person expresses concern about a family member involved with a cult, perhaps the best course of action is to ensure that the person being counseled understands his or her own faith *and* how to communicate that faith to the cultist in an intelligent, loving manner.

18. LeDoux v. LeDoux, 452 N.W.2d 1 (S.Ct. Neb. 1990).

# 16

# Christian Conciliation: An Alternative to Litigation

This book has discussed many legal issues and provided case examples of churches, ministries, and individual pastors and counselors who have been sued for their professional conduct. Not to mince words here, some suits may be justified. When, for example, a pastor or counselor goes beyond the scope of his or her own competencies and harm comes as a direct result of the counseling, when a counselor becomes sexually involved with a client or counselee, when a counselor is in the position to prevent harm from occurring to a third party and neglects to do so, the party who has been harmed may indeed have cause to sue.

There is, however, one problem we have not yet addressed: most personal tort suits against pastors and Christian counselors are filed by other Christians. According to one attorney, referring to civil lawsuits on the whole, one out of five suits involves a Christian taking another Christian to court.[1] Nonetheless, regardless of how legitimate the claims made in the litigation may be, the apostle Paul tells us that Christians shouldn't sue other Christians at all:

> Does any one of you, when he has a case against his neighbor, dare to go to law before the unrighteous, and not before the

1. John Edward Jones, *Reconciliation* (Minneapolis: Bethany House, 1984), p. 149.

> saints? Or do you not know that the saints will judge the world? And if the world is judged by you, are you not competent to constitute the smallest law courts? Do you not know that we shall judge angels? How much more, matters of this life? If then you have law courts dealing with matters of this life, do you appoint them as judges who are of no account in the church? I say this to your shame. Is it so, that there is not among you one wise man who will be able to decide between his brethren, but brother goes to law with brother, and that before unbelievers? Actually, then, it is already a defeat for you, that you have lawsuits with one another. Why not rather be wronged? Why not rather be defrauded? On the contrary, you yourselves wrong and defraud, and that your brethren. (1 Corinthians 6:1-8)

That Christians shouldn't sue each other in secular courts does not lessen the fact that pastoral and counseling professionals should act in a competent and responsible manner in their ministries. Yet in looking at recent trends, it is interesting to note that the development of alternative methods of settling disputes by avoiding civil courts has been led not by Christians but by the secular world.

Over the past decade, the field of Alternative Dispute Resolution (ADR) has gained a stronghold in legal practice in the United States. The primary reason for this, from a secular perspective, is that the court system is so overcrowded that it may take several years for a case to be adjudicated to its conclusion. (Remember, for example, that the *Nally* case was in the court system for more than nine years.) Christians are just beginning to catch up with alternatives to litigation and have developed Christian conciliation ministries that utilize the techniques of alternative dispute resolution within a biblical framework.

Alternative dispute resolution, as practiced in the secular world, involves using negotiation, mediation, and arbitration to settle disputes between parties in conflict. ADR has been used to adjudicate cases between individuals, small businesses, and even large corporations, and its success has proved that disputes need not go through the court system in order to reach settlement.

Traditionally, however, secular ADR has one goal: resolving the dispute. The disadvantage to ADR is that while the legal issues in a case may be successfully resolved without litigation, the opposing parties are not reconciled to each other outside of the ADR arena.

Realizing that this wasn't enough for Christians who wanted to follow a biblical model, several Christian attorneys developed a concept of conciliation designed not only to resolve the dispute itself by using general legal principles applied in a biblical framework but to actually reconcile the opposing parties as members of the Body of Christ. Christian conciliation, then, is based on the biblical model of reconciliation as taught by Jesus: "If therefore you are presenting your offering at the altar, and there remember that your brother has something against you, leave your offering there before the altar, and go your way, first be reconciled to your brother, and then come and present your offering" (Matthew 5:23-24).

Paul elaborates on the theology of reconciliation taught in the New Testament in his second letter to the church at Corinth:

> Therefore if any man is in Christ, he is a new creature; the old things passed away; behold, new things have come. Now all these things are from God, who reconciled us to Himself through Christ, and gave us the ministry of reconciliation, namely, that God was in Christ reconciling the world to Himself, not counting their trespasses against them, and He has committed to us the word of reconciliation. (2 Corinthians 5:17-19)

## Christian Conciliation in Practice

There are presently fifty Christian conciliation ministries operating in the United States and Canada that are part of the Association of Christian Conciliation Services (ACCS).[2]

2. Christian conciliation ministries affiliated with ACCS are located in Alabama, Arizona, California, Colorado, Florida, Georgia, Guam, Illinois, Kansas, Kentucky, Michigan, Minnesota, Missouri, Montana, Nevada, New York, North Carolina, North Dakota, Ohio, Oklahoma, Oregon, Pennsylvania, South Carolina, Tennessee, Texas, Virginia, and Washington. For locations, contact the Association of Christian Conciliation Services, 1537 Avenue D., Suite 352, Billings, MT 59102; telephone: (406) 256-1583.

Additionally, individual denominations have entered the conciliation arena, forming denominational agencies and training programs designed to teach conciliators within the local church. One of the oldest is the Mennonite Conciliation Service, coordinated by the Mennonite Central Committee and jointly sponsored by the Mennonite and Brethren in Christ Churches.

Christian conciliation may involve three steps used in the traditional process of conflict resolution:

> First, one or both parties to a dispute may receive *individual counseling* on how to resolve the dispute in private. Second, if private efforts are unsuccessful, the parties may submit their dispute for *mediation*, which means that one or more mediators will meet with them to promote constructive dialogue and to encourage a voluntary settlement of their differences. Third, if mediation is unsuccessful, the parties may proceed to *arbitration*, which means that one or more arbitrators will hear their case and render a legally binding decision.[3]

Christian counselors, mediators, and arbitrators, all referred to as "conciliators" in the process, may come from a number of professions, including law, ministry, or a profession in which the dispute is centered. (For example, in a dispute centering on the repair of an automobile, the conciliation panel may consist of a lawyer, a pastor, and an experienced mechanic.) All conciliators are expected to be impartial, and do not participate in cases in which they have a vested interest.

In the conciliation process, the general principles of civil law are followed (many of which are based on biblical principles), including the rules of evidence, discovery proceedings, and the submission of legal briefs. But several factors make the conciliation process different from a court trial. These include a stipulation of confidentiality among the participants and, most notably, the assumption that the Bible is the ultimate guide for the resolution of the dispute. Whereas secular

3. C. Ken Sande, *Christian Conciliation: A Better Way to Settle Conflicts* (Billings, Mont.: Association of Christian Conciliation Services, 1989), p. 5.

courts can neither interpret nor admit Scripture into evidence, Christian conciliation can do both.

Can Christian conciliation work? Witness the account of what would normally have been a bitter proceeding in a court of law:

> The two attorneys walked into the room and sat down opposite each other. So did the parents and step-parents of a 10-year-old boy, who, that recent morning, was the center of attention. Both couples wanted custody of the youngster.
>
> This could have been the scene of a bitter court battle, just one of millions of disputes that clog the nation's judicial system each year.
>
> But, from the outset, something was different about this case.
>
> As he introduced the proceeding, Los Angeles lawyer C. Fred Cassity turned to the couples and the boy and said, "As we hear one another today, if we are eloquent and persuasive and do everything right procedurally, but fail to exhibit true love, one for another, the process has failed. The issue today is not 'winning' but determining God's will in this specific case. . . .
>
> "It is primarily this quality that sets these proceedings apart from anything the world can offer."
>
> The custody case was "tried," not in court, but in a church.
>
> The decision was made, not by a judge, but by five church elders.
>
> And instead of charging fees, the attorneys donated their services. Each couple gave a nominal gift to the church.[4]

The same success stories have been told of the Christian conciliation process by parties involved in a wide variety of disputes including business, contract, creditor/debtor, estate, family, employment, landlord/tenant, personal injury, and real estate. Nonetheless, there are several factors that can act against the successful implementation of Christian conciliation in legal disputes.

4. Russell Chandler, "Legal Fights End Up in Church Halls," *Los Angeles Times*, 11 April 1980, p. 1-A. Reprinted in Lynn R. Buzzard and Laurence Eck, *Tell It to the Church* (Elgin, Ill.: David C. Cook, 1982), p. 15.

1. Christian conciliation works only when the opposing parties are both Christian and are both open to the idea of the conciliation process. The process generally does not work with the non-Christian by its very nature, since an unbeliever does not hold Scripture to be an authoritative guide to the resolution of disputes.
2. We are not only Christians but also citizens of a nation that places a high priority on litigation. We may accept Scripture as authoritative and cognitively understand the priority of resolving our differences out of the secular courtroom, yet still be entrapped by a "take them to court" mentality. According to Ronald Kraybill, "One of the toughest problems for peacemakers is bringing disputing parties into a conflict resolution process. Often the same factors which create a dispute cause the disputing parties to resist mediation attempts—fear of conflict, suspicion of motivations, or a genuine belief that discussion will do no good."[5]
3. In the conciliation process, we may use Scripture as a weapon against the party with whom we have a dispute, rather than as an instrument for self-examination. The conciliation session becomes a contest in which we throw "proof texts" at each other instead of making a sincere effort at reconciling as brethren. Even though Scripture admonishes us to be humble and even to take a loss at the expense of winning the case, acknowledging that we should rather be wronged or defrauded (1 Corinthians 6:7), humility is often a bitter pill to swallow.
4. The attorneys who have formed local chapters of the Christian Conciliation Service are sincere and dedicated to the ministry of reconciliation. However, most CCS chapters are part-time ministries for the lawyers who coordinate them. Although their motives are pure, the amount of time needed in such a commitment often takes second place to their full-time legal work.

5. Ronald S. Kraybill, "A Procedure for Mediating Interpersonal Disputes," in *Mediation/Arbitration: A Reader*, ed. Lynn R. Buzzard and Ronald Kraybill (Oak Park, Ill.: Christian Legal Society, 1982).

5. According to one Christian Conciliation Service manual, "The CCS views itself as an arm of the local church and will enter a case only with the approval and cooperation of the church authorities of Christian parties. Our goal is to assist churches as they assume their primary responsibility for the resolution of members' disputes."[6] However, many pastors do not perceive 1 Corinthians 6:1-8 as prohibiting lawsuits between Christians or are otherwise not willing to commit themselves to the conciliation process.

## The Future of Christian Conciliation

The ideal environment in which Christian conciliation can take place is the local church, and the Association of Christian Conciliation Services has designed a comprehensive training program, including clinical supervision, for pastors and laypersons.[7] The organizational concepts of Christian Conciliation Services have only been developed over the last decade or so, and indications are that their strongest potential is in the resolution of interpersonal disputes. Not only should reconciliation be a ministry of the church, it should also play a strong role in the Christian counseling process.

There are no significant case studies in which Christian conciliation has been implemented in a dispute involving a pastor or Christian counselor and a parishioner or client who feels that he or she has been wronged in the process of counseling. Certainly, there should be the potential for conciliation to take place in these situations. However, successful conciliation will likely require that the process be coordinated by a pastor or counselor other than the one involved in the dispute.

The highest priority, though, must be a change in mindset, a moving away from "The People's Court" mentality that

6. C. Ken Sande, *Peacemaker's Handbook*, rev. 5.3 (Merrifield, Va.: Christian Legal Society, n.d.), p. 12.
7. For information on the ACCS Conciliator Training Program, see the *Association of Christian Conciliation Services Membership Manual* (Billings, Mont.: Association of Christian Conciliation Services, 1990).

says when you have a dispute with your neighbor, "Don't take matters into your own hands; take them to court." Secular society may give us that option, but the Word of God does not.

# 17

# Legal Resources for Christian Counselors

A few years ago, while I was pursuing my masters degree in theology and law, I often utilized the resources at the library of a local law school. Late one evening, as I was doing research in the proverbial "lower stacks," I came across someone who looked like a lost boy in a department store. He explained that he was a student in the Masters of Business Administration program at the university with which the law school was affiliated and that he was required to write a paper dealing with trademark infringement. Coming across some legal references, he decided to attempt to find the cases and read the opinions.

His "lost boy" attitude was based not only on the fact that this was his first time in a law library but also on a perception implanted in his mind by the professor who had assigned the paper, a practicing attorney who served as an adjunct faculty member in the university's business program. The professor had told his class that they shouldn't bother checking the law library for resources, since they would understand neither how to use the library nor how to read case opinions.

We spent the next fifteen minutes together, and the business student left with an understanding of how to utilize law library resources that was better than I've seen in most students at the law school itself. The primary problem with most people's understanding (or misunderstanding) of legal issues is a perception that's often caused by attorneys themselves—that the law is a noble topic kept on such a high pedestal that no one but a lawyer could possibly understand it. Nothing could be further from the truth.

## Law, Social Grace, and Public Perception

The practice of law is based on an adversarial relationship. Cases are often won, not on the merits of which side is right or wrong, but on which side has the better attorney (or on which attorney can better convince a judge or jury of the client's cause). Unlike physicians, many of whom tend to socialize only with other physicians, lawyers are more open about socializing with nonlawyers. A reason for this is that attorneys who socialize with each other one evening are likely to face each other from an adversarial position the following morning. Unlike physicians, who are dedicated to winning the battle over an impersonal disease, attorneys are in battle against each other in courts of law.

At the same time, there is a mystique to the study and practice of law that lawyers perpetuate with the nonattorney. The American court system, largely based on the system of English common law, is steeped in ceremony, and this tradition continues today, even in the heat of courtroom battle.

As a nonattorney who has had to deal with the prejudice of lawyers toward outsiders who enter the inner sanctum, I have become convinced that there are essentially two types of attorneys practicing today. The first is the type of person who recognizes that the law is, in the words of the *Declaration of Independence*, "of the people, by the people, and for the people" and has no compulsion against the nonattorney knowing as much about a legal issue as he or she does. The other type of attorney is the one who places the law (and the lawyer) on a pedestal and resists the exploration of legal issues by a nonattorney. I have been blessed to deal with and enjoy fellowship with the first type of attorney for several years now, and I can assure the reader that the law is not only understandable by the layperson, it is a fascinating area of study by theologically oriented persons.

A caveat is appropriate here regarding the unauthorized practice of law by nonattorneys. All states have statutes dealing with the practice of law, which is generally held to include the following: (1) the representation of others before judicial or administrative bodies; (2) advising others on their legal problems regularly and for a fee; and (3) the drafting of legal instruments. Only attorneys licensed by a local or state bar association for a given jurisdiction may engage in these practices.

There are exceptions to the rule, the most common of which is *appearance pro se*, i.e., a person defending his or her own suit personally and without counsel. (This is not a recommended practice. Most people are familiar with the old expression "The attorney who defends himself has a fool for a client.") Some states have other exceptions, including representation by laypersons before particular courts (such as justice of the peace courts or small claims courts), a corporation attending to its own business, the recognition of nonresident attorneys (i.e., those who practice in jurisdictions other than where a case is being heard), and some representation of charitable and benevolent associations.[1]

## IMPLICATIONS FOR PASTORS AND COUNSELORS

The bottom line is that, despite all of the information contained in this book about legal issues, when it comes down to a potential lawsuit, you will need a competent attorney to guide you through the maze of the legal system. Having read this volume, you now know more than the average attorney about how the law impacts Christian counselors.

1. See, e.g., Justine Fischer and Dorothy H. Lachmann, *Unauthorized Practice Handbook* (Chicago: American Bar Association, 1972; Buffalo: William S. Hein & Co., 1990), pp. 15-35. For our purposes, two recommendations are appropriate: first, in a legal proceeding, pastors and counselors should be represented by competent attorneys (after all, a little knowledge of the law can be worse than none at all if it results in a person's being tempted to self-representation); second, the pastor or counselor should take care not to engage in unauthorized practice by representing, advising, or drafting instruments for other persons in a legal context.

Nonetheless, the legal system tends to be a world of its own, with walls that reach high, and this volume is no substitute for competent legal representation.

There is, however, the matter of *choosing* an attorney. While you will want the most competent person possible representing you in a court of law, you won't want to be stuck with the type of lawyer who refuses to explain the ramifications of a legal issue because "you won't understand it."

If you have such an attorney, there are two ways to deal with the situation. One is to find another attorney. The other is to establish at the beginning of the legal relationship that you, as a pastor or counselor, operate on the same professional level as the attorney, albeit in a different field. The most important consideration: Do not accept the myth that the law cannot be competently understood by anyone but a lawyer.

As discussed in chapter 2, one of the main problems in litigation affecting the Christian church is that few attorneys are trained in the nature of religious case law in the course of their legal education. Therefore, whether he or she admits it or not, handling a lawsuit with religious implications will be just as much an education for the attorney as it is for any other party to the suit.

If you are sued, you have an opportunity, as a consumer of legal services, to take the initiative in aiding your attorney with the legal process as he or she represents you. Not only will this make you a better counseling practitioner in future cases, it can save you a significant amount of money in legal fees. This chapter, a crash course in legal research, is designed to help you in that department.

## THE KEY TO UNDERSTANDING CASE REFERENCES

Each legal case referenced in this book, as in any volume dealing with the law, is referenced (or, in legal terms, *cited*) by the law book or "reporter" in which the opinion appears. The *Nally* case, for example, is cited as

> Nally v. Grace Community Church of the Valley, 763 P.2d 948 (S.Ct. Cal. 1988).

The citation indicates the case name, volume number, law book (reporter), page, court, and year the case was decided. In the *Nally* example, the case opinion may be found in volume 763 of the Pacific Reporter, 2d series, beginning on page 948. The case was decided by the Supreme Court of California in 1988.

All case citations follow the same format, except that Supreme Court citations omit the name of the Court since all cases reported in a Supreme Court reporter come from that Court. For example, the case of *Reynolds v. United States*, 98 U.S. 145 (1878), appears in volume 98 of the United States Reporter, beginning on page 145, and the case was decided in 1878.

## FEDERAL CASE CITATIONS

United States Supreme Court cases appear in three different resources:

United States Reports (abbreviated *U.S.*)
Supreme Court Reporter (abbreviated *S.Ct.*)
United States Supreme Court Reports, Lawyers' Edition (abbreviated *L.Ed.*)

The three Supreme Court reporters essentially duplicate each other (though they are printed by different publishers), but such is the nature of the legal profession.[2]

The reporters are published once enough opinions are released to fill an entire volume and may not be published until several months after the Supreme Court decides a case. However, Supreme Court opinions also appear in a publication called *U.S. Law Week* (abbreviated *U.S.L.W.*), which is print-

2. *United States Reports* is the official reporter of the United States Supreme Court and is published by the U.S. Government Printing Office (Washington, D.C.). The *Supreme Court Reporter*, published by West Publishing Company (St. Paul, Minn.), is also commonly cited because it is published earlier than the official reporter. It is also used extensively by many attorneys to cross-reference cases by issue or area of law. *Supreme Court Reports, Lawyer's Edition*, published by the Lawyers Cooperative Publishing Company (Rochester, N.Y.), is the least referenced of the three.

ed within forty-eight hours of the decision. Therefore, if a significant case is decided and you want to read the opinion before it is published in the permanent reporter, it will usually be available at your local law library in *U.S.L.W.* within a week of its release.

Another immediate resource for court opinions is an on-line computer network that may be found in some lawyers' offices. The two most common networks, *LEXIS* and *Westlaw,* are similar to on-line networks available to the general public (such as *CompuServe* or *Prodigy*). However, the cost is much more expensive. *CompuServe* charges as little as six dollars per hour for on-line time, whereas the cost of using a legal computer network can approach three hundred dollars per hour. Even though the legal computer networks charge an exorbitant rate, this is not a major concern to attorneys, who simply pass the cost on to the client as a charge for legal research.

Cases decided by the U.S. Court of Appeals appear in the *Federal Reporter, Second Series* (abbreviated *F.2d*); cases from federal district courts are published in the *Federal Supplement* (abbreviated *F.Supp.*). Legal cases work their way upward through the federal system. A case may first be heard in a district court, then appealed to the U.S. Court of Appeals, and finally to the U.S. Supreme Court. (On occasion, cases that pose a substantive constitutional question move directly from the district court to the Supreme Court.)

By way of example, the case of *United States v. Ballard* was heard in all three courts, and the resulting opinions appear in different reporters:

- *United States v. Ballard,* 35 F.Supp. 105 (S.D. Cal. 1940). Here the case was heard in the federal district court for the southern district of California, and the opinion was published in volume 35 of the Federal Supplement in the year 1940, beginning on p. 105.
- *United States v. Ballard,* 138 F.2d 540 (9th Cir. 1943). Here the case was heard in the U.S. Court of Appeals, 9th Circuit, and the opinion was published in volume 138 of the Federal Reporter, 2d Series, in 1943, beginning on p. 540.

- *United States v. Ballard,* 322 U.S. 78 (1944). Here the case was heard by the U.S. Supreme Court, and the opinion was published in volume 322 of the United States Reports in 1944, beginning on p. 78.

When, in a footnote or reference, two page numbers are indicated, the first number indicates the first page of the opinion, and the second number indicates the page from which the quote or reference was taken. In the case of *United States v. Ballard,* for example, the reference *322 U.S. 78, 81 (1944)* indicates that whereas the opinion begins on p. 78 of the reporter, the cited material may be found on p. 81 of the reporter.

## STATE CASE CITATIONS

Nonfederal citations may be found in a series of regional reporters that are published for the state courts around the nation:

| Abbreviation | Reporter |
| --- | --- |
| A.2d | Atlantic Reporter, 2d Series |
| P.2d | Pacific Reporter, 2d Series |
| N.E.2d | Northeast Reporter, 2d Series |
| N.W.2d | Northwest Reporter, 2d Series |
| So.2d | Southern Reporter, 2d Series |

In addition to the regional reporter, a case may also appear in a reporter issued within an individual state. State Supreme Court cases published in the Pacific Reporter, for example, also appear in the California Reporter. Though this, again, is a duplication, all law libraries maintain the complete set of regional reporters in their holdings, while they usually maintain the individual state reporter only for their own or adjacent states.

## LAW LIBRARIES: A "USER-FRIENDLY" RESOURCE

Law libraries are maintained by all ABA-approved law schools. Many of them act as federal document repositories and, as such, are required to be open to the public for use. Acting as a repository for government documents simply means that the library maintains holdings of federal documents such as congressional proceedings, the Federal Register (a compilation of administrative and legislative acts), and other government documents.

Whereas law school libraries must be open to the public, they may *reasonably* restrict public access. This usually means that members of the public do not have borrowing privileges. This is insignificant, however, since most of the legal volumes you, as a pastor or counselor, will be interested in do not circulate outside of the library at all.

Other reasonable restrictions of public access may include limiting the hours the library is open to the public or limiting access to the library during specified times of the year (e.g., before mid-term or final examinations). Law school libraries that are part of major universities or are located in large cities often have more restrictive policies than those in smaller towns due to more extensive use.

Most areas of the country also have city or county law libraries, usually located in a local county court house. As tax-supported libraries, these are also generally open to the public, though borrowing privileges may be restricted to attorneys who belong to the local bar association. (Again, an inconvenience that's not very significant since even attorneys can't borrow legal reporters.)

In addition to legal reporters, one of the most useful resources of the law library will be law reviews (professional journals published by most law schools). Issues are covered in law review articles more thoroughly than they are in general newspapers, and current cases are cross-referenced to related cases that have been heard in the past. Law libraries located at law schools usually have a better selection of law reviews than county law libraries, as well as the advantage of charging less for photocopies. (County law libraries usually charge twenty-five cents per copy—a high cost, but attorneys who make copies at county law libraries usually pass the cost on to their clients.)

Many law school libraries also have a *LegalTrac* computer, a user-friendly system that will print out a list of relevant law review articles based on subject or case name. The user simply types in a topic (e.g., *clergy malpractice*), and the computer prints a list of law review articles dealing with the subject requested. The *LegalTrac* computer is similar to the *InfoTrac* system that can be found in many public libraries, but it is specifically geared toward legal topics.

In short, law school libraries are better equipped, charge less for photocopies, and have longer daily hours. (During the school year, many of them are open seven days a week until midnight.) For persons living in rural areas or far from a law school, county libraries may not offer the same convenience of hours or selection of law reviews, but they are more than adequate for case research.

Law school libraries are generally staffed by students (especially during the evening hours), and they are usually very helpful in pointing the novice in the right direction. Law librarians are also an excellent resource, and most of them are cooperative about helping nonlawyers find the information they are seeking. In county law libraries, you may encounter a little more resistance, since the librarians are used to dealing primarily with practicing attorneys. Remember, however, that you can catch more flies with honey than with vinegar, and that you, as a taxpayer, do have the right to use the county law library as a resource.

## General Reading in Christianity and the Law

Several good books deal with the impact of law on religious issues (some of which are cited in the bibliography at the end of this book). Within this chapter, I would especially recommend two of them for pastors and counselors.

*The Christian Legal Advisor*, by John Eidsmoe,[3] deals with legal issues affecting both churches and individual Christians today and includes a comprehensive background study on constitutional issues that affect the religious rights

3. John Eidsmoe, *The Christian Legal Advisor*, rev. ed. (Grand Rapids: Baker, 1987).

of believers. Eidsmoe, a legal scholar and constitutional law professor, provides one of the most comprehensive analyses of legal thinking available today, and this book will inform the reader of how courts adjudicate cases from a philosophical perspective.

*Pastor, Church, and Law*, by Richard Hammar,[4] deals with legal issues specifically affecting individual pastors and churches. Hammar, who serves as general counsel for the Assemblies of God denomination, does not cover constitutional theory but provides extensive information on issues such as taxation and church administration.

The reader should note, however, that legal trends change. The *Nally* case, for example, may be the predominant precedent in the area of "clergy malpractice" today, but a future ruling could change the picture significantly. (Witness, for example, the immediate change in legal thinking on the abortion issue that came after the *Roe v. Wade* decision in 1973.)

There are also periodicals geared toward persons in ministry that are designed to provide updates on legal issues affecting Christians, but these tend to be very expensive and a month or two behind the times.[5] However, popular publications such as *Christianity Today*, *Moody* magazine, and *Charisma and Christian Life* generally cover legal issues in brief. Interested persons can then read relevant case opinions at their local law library.

## ORGANIZATIONAL RESOURCES

Finally, several organizations exist that specifically defend Christian churches and organizations in religious cases. These include the Christian Law Association,[6] the Christian

4. Richard R. Hammar, *Pastor, Church, and Law* (Springfield, Mo.: Gospel Publishing, 1983).
5. These include *The Religious Freedom Reporter*, published monthly by the Campbell University School of Law (Buies Creek, N.C.), which costs ninety-five dollars per year, and *Church Law and Tax Report*, published six times a year by Christian Ministry Resources (Matthews, N.C.), which costs seventy-eight dollars per year.
6. The Christian Law Association, P.O. Box 30, Conneaut, OH 44030; telephone: (216) 593-3933. CLA is a nonprofit ministry affiliated with a law firm in Ohio and primarily deals with cases involving the freedom of church schools to operate without federal or state regulation.

Legal Society,[7] the National Legal Foundation,[8] the Rutherford Institute,[9] and the Western Center for Law and Religious Freedom.[10] As public-interest law firms, these organizations are nonprofit corporations and are exempt under Sec. 501(c)(3) of the Internal Revenue Code. The problem with any nonprofit legal organization, however, is that the cases they accept usually involve high-profile issues that can be utilized in their fund-raising efforts.[11] Thus, they may not accept an individual case that does not have constitutional implications. There are exceptions to every rule, however, and they can be consulted in the event that you need an attorney and do not have one.

7. The Christian Legal Society, P.O. Box 1492, Merrifield, VA 22003; telephone: (703) 642-1070. CLS is primarily a fellowship and networking organization for Christian attorneys; they do not litigate cases, but have filed some *amici curae* ("friend-of-the-court" briefs) in significant federal cases.
8. The National Legal Foundation, P.O. Box D, Chesapeake, VA 23320-0020; telephone: (804) 424-4242. NLF handles primarily First Amendment cases, specializing in issues centering on religious expression in public schools. Although they are not engaged in counseling issues per se, they do have an attorney referral network for Christians seeking help with religion-oriented legal issues.
9. The Rutherford Institute, P.O. Box 8482, Charlottesville, VA 22906-7482; telephone: (804) 978-3888. The Rutherford Institute handles cases primarily of a constitutional nature (e.g., school prayer, equal access, freedom to evangelize).
10. The Western Center for Law and Religious Freedom, 1211 "H" Street, Suite A, Sacramento, CA 95814; telephone: (916) 447-4111. The only major public interest law firm dealing with Christian legal issues on the Pacific coast, the center focuses on fundamental constitutional and legal principles throughout the western states.
11. An example of how Christian legal organizations, most of which are nonprofit, use high-profile cases for fund-raising purposes can be found by looking at the case of *Board of Education of the Westside Community Schools v. Mergens*, 110 S.Ct. 2356 (1990). In June 1990, the U.S. Supreme Court upheld the constitutionality of the Equal Access Act, 42 U.S.C. 2071 (1984), which grants students the right to form religious clubs in public high schools. Shortly after the decision, several Christian legal organizations mailed fund-raising appeals in which they took credit for winning the case. These included Christian Advocates Serving Evangelism, the Christian Legal Society, National Legal Foundation, and the Rutherford Institute. The case was actually argued before the Supreme Court by Jay Sekulow, a constitutional attorney with Christian Advocates Serving Evangelism in Atlanta, Georgia. However, Sekulow worked with the National Legal Foundation, which had taken the case before the federal district and appeals courts. The Christian Legal Society and the Rutherford Institute filed *amicus curae* (friend-of-the-court) briefs but otherwise took no part in the case.

## Some Final Words

There is no defense in terms of being sued by a person who intentionally wants to cause a legal problem for your pastoral or counseling ministry. If you or your church are sued, chances are good that you will be able to win the case (assuming you acted in a professional and responsible manner in your dealings with the plaintiff). However, the process of defense is a costly one in terms of time, energy, and money.

There are, however, several steps you can take to minimize your risk of being sued and to help you deal with the potential for litigation in the future.

1. Pray. I've mentioned this peripherally in other areas, but let's face it—prayer is perhaps the most important part of your counseling work. If you're not in touch with God's will for your ministry, you shouldn't be involved in a ministry endeavor until you are.
2. Be, in the words of Jay Adams, as *competent to counsel* as possible. God does not dictate that every pastor or Christian counselor have a doctorate degree in counseling, nor that formal education is the most important component in terms of being a good counselor. The Lord doesn't lead everyone to become an authority in the counseling field, but Scripture does indicate that within the scope and content of the ministry you are pursuing, you should be "handling accurately the word of truth" (2 Timothy 2:15). Ongoing training, whether in a formal environment or through independent study, can be a valuable asset.
3. Find an attorney competent in dealing with religious issues and with whom you feel comfortable *before* you need one. If you are threatened with a lawsuit, time and pressure at that point may keep you from seeking the best legal representation for your case. This does not mean choosing a deacon or elder in your church who happens to be a lawyer, or a friend or relative (who may be a good general lawyer but does not have a competent knowledge of religious issues); it means choosing the best lawyer for your specific needs.

4. If you are a pastor, you should consider carrying clergy malpractice insurance. Even though the *Nally* court established that there is no such tort as clergy malpractice per se, malpractice insurance will pay much of your defense fees if you are sued for counseling malpractice or negligence. Clergy malpractice insurance is often available as a low-cost rider to your church's existing policy.
5. If you are a pastor of a small church or have a private counseling practice, seek the fellowship of one or more other local pastors or counselors for mutual support in your ministry. Christianity all too often becomes a "one-person show," and lack of fellowship with someone in whom you can confide may result in making a poor counseling decision in your own ministry.

This is the "end of the book." I cannot make assurances as authoritative as those in Scripture, but I hope I'm right when I say that if we exhibit due care in our ministries, counting the cost as we enter the field, we *will* win.

# Bibliography

Adams, Jay E. *Competent to Counsel.* Phillipsburg, N.J.: Presbyterian & Reformed, 1970.

———. *Handbook of Church Discipline.* Grand Rapids: Zondervan, 1986.

Amos, William E., Jr., "When AIDS Comes to Church." *Leadership,* Fall 1989, pp. 66-73.

*Association of Christian Conciliation Services Membership Manual.* Billings, Mont.: Association of Christian Conciliation Services, 1990.

Baker, Don. *Beyond Forgiveness: The Healing Touch of Church Discipline.* Portland: Multnomah, 1984.

Barron, Bruce. *The Health and Wealth Gospel.* Downers Grove, Ill.: InterVarsity, 1987.

Basil, Robert J. "Clergy Malpractice: Taking Spiritual Counseling Conflicts Beyond Intentional Tort Analysis." *Rutgers Law Journal* 19 (1988): 419-50.

Bear, John. *Bear's Guide to Earning Non-Traditional College Degrees,* 10th ed. Berkeley, Calif.: Ten Speed, 1988.

Beck, James C., ed. *The Potentially Violent Patient and the Tarasoff Decision in Psychiatric Practice.* Washington, D.C.: American Psychiatric, 1985.

Bobgan, Martin, and Deidre Bobgan. *Prophets of Psychoheresy I.* Santa Barbara, Calif.: East Gate, 1989.

Bork, Robert H. *The Tempting of America: The Political Seduction of the Law.* New York: The Free Press, 1990.

Boyle, Beth Ellen, ed. *Words of Conscience: Religious Statements on Conscientious Objection,* 10th ed. Washington, D.C.: National Interreligious Service Board for Conscientious Objectors, 1983.

Buzzard, Lynn. "Scarlet Letter Lawsuits: Private Affairs and Public Judgments." *Campbell Law Review* 10 (1987): 1-68.

Buzzard, Lynn R., and Thomas S. Brandon, Jr. *Church Discipline and the Courts.* Wheaton, Ill.: Tyndale, 1987.

Buzzard, Lynn R., and Laurence Eck. *Tell It to the Church.* Elgin, Ill.: David C. Cook, 1982.

Carlson, Lee W. *Child Sexual Abuse: A Handbook for Clergy and Church Members.* Valley Forge, Pa.: Judson, 1988.

*CCCO Military Counselor's Manual.* Philadelphia: Central Committee for Conscientious Objectors, n.d.

Chandler, Russell. "Legal Fights End Up in Church Halls." *Los Angeles Times*, 11 April 1980, p. 1-A. Reprinted in Lynn R. Buzzard and Laurence Eck, *Tell It to the Church.* Elgin, Ill.: David C. Cook, 1982.

Cohen, Cynthia B. "Birth of a Network." *Hastings Center Report*, February-March 1988, p. 11.

Collins, Gary R. *Christian Counseling: A Comprehensive Guide.* Waco, Tex.: Word, 1980.

Coyle, Marcia. "How Americans View High Court." *The National Law Journal* 26, February 1990, pp. 1, 36-37.

Danchi, Theodore S. "Church Discipline on Trial: Religious Freedom Versus Individual Privacy." *Valparaiso University Law Review* 21 (1987): 387-429.

Davis, John Jefferson. *Evangelical Ethics.* Phillipsburg, N.J.: Presbyterian and Reformed, 1985.

Davis, Karen, and Diane Rowland, *Medicare Policy: New Directions for Health and Long-Term Care.* Baltimore: The Johns Hopkins University Press, 1986.

"The Death of Liberty?" *The Briefcase* (newsletter of the Christian Law Association), July 1990, pp. 1, 6.

Eidsmoe, John. *The Christian Legal Advisor*, rev. ed. Grand Rapids: Baker, 1987.

Enroth, Ronald. *A Guide to Cults and New Religions.* Downers Grove, Ill.: InterVarsity, 1983.

Fischer, Justine, and Dorothy H. Lachmann. *Unauthorized Practice Handbook.* Chicago: American Bar Association, 1972. Reprint. Buffalo: William S. Hein & Co., 1990.

Fogarty, John P. C. "The Right Not to Kill: A Critical Analysis of Conscientious Objection and the Problem of Registration." *New England Law Review* 18 (1985): 655-86.

Frame, Randy. "AIDS: Coming to a Church Near You." *Christianity Today*, 18 June 1990, pp. 50-52.

Galanter, Mark. *Cults: Faith, Healing, and Coercion.* New York: Oxford University Press, 1989.

Galvin, Bill, and Larry Spears. "Selective Service Proposes New Regulations." *CCCO News Notes*, Winter 1981, p. 1.

Groth, A. Nicholas, Robert E. Longo, and J. Bradley McFadin. "Undetected Recidivism Among Rapists and Child Molesters." *Crime & Delinquency* 28 (1982): 450-58.

Hammar, Richard R. *Pastor, Church & Law.* Springfield, Mo.: Gospel Publishing, 1983.

_______. "Tort and Religion—The American Bar Association Conference on Church Litigation," *Church Law & Tax Report*, July-August 1990, pp. 2-5.

Hammett, Jenny Yates. "A Second Drink at the Well: Theological and Philosophical Content of CPE Origins." *Journal of Pastoral Care* 29 (June 1975): 86-89.

Heroux, Christopher S. "When Fundamental Rights Collide: Guinn v. Collinsville Church of Christ." *Tulsa Law Journal* (1985): 157-82.

Hopkins, Bruce R., and Barbara S. Anderson. *The Counselor and the Law.* Alexandria, Va.: AACD Press, 1985.

House, H. Wayne, ed. *Restoring the Constitution, 1787-1987: Essays in Celebration of the Bicentennial*. Dallas: Probe, 1987.

Hummel, Dean L., Lou C. Talbott, and M. David Alexander. *Law and Ethics in Counseling.* New York: Van Nostrand Reinhold, 1985.

Ivers, William N. "When Must a Priest Report Under a Child Abuse Reporting Statute? Resolution to the Priests' Conflicting Duties." *Valparaiso University Law Review* 21 (1987): 431-65.

Jacquet, Constant H., ed. *Yearbook of American & Canadian Churches, 1990.* Nashville: Abingdon, 1990.

Jones, John Edward. *Reconciliation.* Minneapolis: Bethany House, 1984.

Keiser, Thomas, and Jacqueline Keiser. *The Anatomy of Illusion.* Springfield, Ill.: Charles C. Thomas, 1987.

Kraybill, Ronald S. "A Procedure for Mediating Interpersonal Disputes." In *Mediation/Arbitration: A Reader*, ed. Lynn R. Buzzard and Ronald Kraybill (Oak Park, Ill.: Christian Legal Society, 1982).

Laney, J. Carl. *A Guide to Church Discipline.* Minneapolis: Bethany House, 1985.

Larson, Bob. *Larson's Book of Cults*, rev. ed. Wheaton, Ill.: Tyndale, 1989.

Larson, David B., et al. "Systematic Analysis of Research on Religious Variables in Four Major Psychiatric Journals, 1978-1982." *American Journal of Psychiatry* 143 (March 1986): 329-34.

Lawson, Steve. "The AIDS Debate: An Interview with C. Everett Koop." *Charisma & Christian Life,* June 1989, pp. 72-77.

Macklin, Ruth. "The Inner Workings of an Ethics Committee: Latest Battle over Jehovah's Witnesses." *Hastings Center Report,* February-March 1988, pp. 15-20.

Maresca, Charles A., Jr., ed. *NISBCO Draft Counselors Manual,* 5th ed. Washington, D.C.: National Interreligious Service Board for Conscientious Objectors, 1989.

Martin, Walter. *The Rise of the Cults.* Santa Ana, Calif.: Vision House, 1980.

Miller, Arthur. *Miller's Court.* Boston: Houghton Mifflin, 1982.

Milne, Terry Wuester. "Bless Me, Father, for I Am About to Sin . . . Should Clergy Counselors Have a Duty to Protect Third Parties?" *Tulsa Law Journal* 22 (1986): 139-65.

Mitchell, Mary Harter. "Must Clergy Tell? Child Abuse Reporting Requirements Versus the Clergy Privilege and Free Exercise of Religion." *Minnesota Law Review* 71 (1987): 723-825.

Narramore, Clyde M. *The Psychology of Counseling.* Grand Rapids: Zondervan, 1960.

Pace, Dale K. *A Chaplain's Guide to Effective Jail and Prison Ministries.* Old Tappan, N.J.: Fleming H. Revell, 1973.

Payne, Franklin E., Jr. *Biblical Medical Ethics: The Christian and the Practice of Medicine.* Milford, Mich.: Mott Media, 1985.

Phillips, Michael E. "Helping the Sexually Abused." *Leadership* 10, no. 3: 64-71.

Sande, C. Ken. *Peacemaker's Handbook,* rev. 5.3. Merrifield, Va.: Christian Legal Society, n.d.

———. *Christian Conciliation: A Better Way to Settle Conflicts.* Billings, Mont.: Association of Christian Conciliation Services, 1989.

Sharpe, J. Shelby. "The Coming Nuclear Attack on Christianity in America: A Report on the American Bar Association Seminar *Tort and Religion.*" Fort Worth: Sharpe, Bates & McGee, 1989.

Sherman, Rorie. "Legal Spotlight on Priests Who Are Pedophiles." *The National Law Journal,* 4 April 1988, pp. 1, 28-29.

Slind-Flor, Victoria. "At the Limits: Major AIDS Cases Have Been Teaching Old Law New Tricks." *The National Law Journal,* 27 August 1990, pp. 1, 31-32.

Smolla, Rodney A. *Jerry Falwell v. Larry Flynt: The First Amendment on Trial.* New York: St. Martins, 1988.

Spring, Beth, and Ed Larson. *Euthanasia: Spiritual, Medical & Legal Issues in Terminal Health Care.* Portland: Multnomah, 1988.

Sweeney, Gail White. "Conscientious Objection and the First Amendment." *Akron Law Review* 14 (1980): 71-84.

Terry, Randall. *Operation Rescue.* Springdale, Pa.: Whitaker House, 1988.

Troyer, Robert C. "Protecting the Flock from the Shepherd: A Duty of Care and Licensing Requirement for Clergy Counselors." *Boston College Law Review* 30 (1989): 1179-1220.

Tucker, Ruth A. *Another Gospel: Alternative Religions and the New Age Movement.* Grand Rapids: Academie Books, 1989.

Veroneau, John K. "In re Gardner: Withdrawing Medical Care from Persistently Vegetative Patients." *Maine Law Review* 41 (1989), pp. 447-65.

Watson, William. *A Concise Dictionary of Cults and Religions.* Chicago: Moody, 1991.

Wright, Stuart A. *Leaving Cults: The Dynamics of Defection.* Washington, D.C.: Society for the Scientific Study of Religion, 1987.

Wuthnow, Robert. *The Struggle for America's Soul.* Grand Rapids: Eerdmans, 1989.

Youngstrom, Nina. "Malpractice Premiums Jump 50 Percent Aug. 1." *APA Monitor,* August 1990, p. 16.

# Cases Cited

Armes v. City of Philadelphia, 706 F.Supp. 1156 (E.D. Pa. 1989).

Board of Education of Nassau County v. Arline, 107 S.Ct. 1123 (1987).

Board of Education of the Westside Community Schools v. Mergens, 110 S.Ct. 2356 (1990).

Bobo v. Texas, 757 S.W.2d 58 (Tex. App. 1988), *cert. denied,* 109 S.Ct. 2066 (1989).

Bunn v. North Carolina, 336 U.S. 942 (1949).

Canon v. Thumudo, 422 N.W. 2d 688 (S.Ct. Mich. 1988).

Chalk v. U.S. District Court, 840 F.2d 701 (9th Cir. 1988).

Cruzan v. Missouri, 110 S.Ct. 2841 (1990).

Currie v. United States, 644 F.Supp. 1074 (M.D.N.C. 1986).

Davis v. Lihm, 335 N.W.2d 481 (Mich. App. 1983).

DeStefano v. Grabian, 763 P.2d 275 (S.Ct. Colo. 1988).

Employment Division, Oregon Department of Human Resources, v. Smith, 110 S.Ct. 1595 (1990).

Erickson v. Christenson, 781 P.2d 383 (Or. App. 1989).

Funkhouser v. Oklahoma, 763 P.2d 695 (Okla. Crim. 1988), *cert. denied* 109 S.Ct. 2066 (1989).

Gillette v. United States, 407 U.S. 437 (1971).

Girouard v. United States, 328 U.S. 61 (1946).

Griswold v. Connecticut, 381 U.S. 479 (1965).

Guinn v. Church of Christ of Collinsville, 775 P.2d 766 (S.Ct. Okla. 1989).

Hester v. Barnett, 723 S.W.2d 544 (Mo. App. 1987).

Hodgson v. Minnesota, 110 S.Ct. 2926 (1990).

Hopewell v. Adibempe, No. GD78-82756, Civil Division, Court of Common Pleas of Allegheny County, Pennsylvania, June 1, 1981.

Hustler Magazine and Larry C. Flynt v. Jerry Falwell, 485 U.S. 46 (1988).

In re Gregory, 515 N.E.2d 286 (Ill. App. 1987).

Jeffrey Scott E. v. Central Baptist Church, 197 Cal. App. 3d (1988).

John Does 1-9 v. Compcare, Inc., 763 P.2d 1237 (Wash. App. 1988).

Katz v. Superior Court, 73 Cal. App. 3d 952 (1977).

LeDoux v. LeDoux, 452 N.W.2d 1 (S.Ct. Neb. 1990).

Lemon v. Kurtzman, 403 U.S. 602 (1971).

Lucy v. State, 443 So.2d 1335 (Crim. App. Ala. 1983).

N.E. Women's Center v. McMonagle, 868 F.2d 1342 (3d Cir. 1989), *cert. denied* 110 S.Ct. 261 (1989).

Nally v. Grace Community Church of the Valley, 763 P.2d 948 (S.Ct. Cal. 1988).

Ohio v. Akron Center for Reproductive Health, 110 S.Ct. 2972 (1990).

Peck v. Counseling Service of Addison County, 499 A.2d 422, (S.Ct. Vt. 1985).

People v. Hodges, No. 614153 (Cal. App. Dept. Super. Ct. 1989).

Peterson v. Sorlien, 299 N.W.2d 123 (S.Ct. Minn. 1980).

Presbyterian Church (U.S.A.) v. United States, 870 F.2d 518 (9th Cir. 1989).

Public Health Trust of Dade County v. Wons, 541 So.2d 96 (S.Ct. Fla. 1989).

Reynolds v. United States, 98 U.S. 145 (1878).

Roe v. Wade, 410 U.S. 113 (1973).

Rostker v. Goldberg, 453 U.S. 57 (1981).

St. Luke Evangelical Church v. Smith, 568 A.2d 35 (S.Ct. Md. 1990).

Sherbert v. Verner, 374 U.S. 398 (1963).

Sicurella v. United States, 345 U.S. 385 (1955).

Sterling v. Bloom, 723 P.2d 755 (S.Ct. Iowa 1986).

Strock v. Pressnell, 527 N.E.2d 1235, 1239 (S.Ct. Ohio, 1988).

Tarasoff v. Board of Regents of the University of California, 551 P.2d 334 (S.Ct. Cal. 1976).

Thompson v. County of Alameda, 614 P.2d 728 (S.Ct. Cal. 1980).

United States v. Aguilar, 871 F.2d 1436 (9th Cir. 1989), *superseded* 883 F.2d 662 (9th Cir. 1989).

United States v. Ballard, 322 U.S. 78 (1944).

United States v. Macintosh, 283 U.S. 605 (1931).

Watson v. Jones, 80 U.S. (13 Wall.) 679 (1872).

Wayte v. United States, 105 S.Ct. 1524 (1985).

Moody Press, a ministry of the Moody Bible Institute,
is designed for education, evangelization, and edification.
If we may assist you in knowing more about Christ
and the Christian life, please write us without obligation:
Moody Press, c/o MLM, Chicago, Illinois 60610.

Webster v. Missouri, 109 S.Ct. 3040 (1989).
Wisconsin v. Yoder, 406 U.S. 205 (1972).